Signing with a heavy hand and heart, Love Mommy

A FAMILY'S JOURNEY THROUGH
FETAL ALCOHOL SYNDROME

Co-authored by
Sondra Torres and Chanel Torres

*"Put love into any situation
and you could divert all
problems."*

John Russell Patronic

1967-2012

Signing with a heavy hand and heart, Love Mommy

A FAMILY'S JOURNEY THROUGH
FETAL ALCOHOL SYNDROME

Co-authored by
Sondra Torres and Chanel Torres

— Tampa, Florida —

John recited this powerful message to Chanel,
"Put love into any situation and you could divert all problems."

This book is dedicated to

John and his dog, Jingo

John Russell Patronie
(Chanel's cousin)
a well known, award winning photographer
in the Miami Beach area and beyond.

February 24, 1967-December 10, 2012
Google "John Patronie"
to view his awesome photography work.

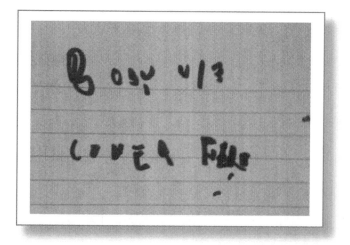

Three months prior to his premature death, he made a promise to Chanel " I would be honored to design your book cover" he proclaimed. His promise carried through to his death bed where he frantically attempted to put it all together before his passing. Although he was to ill to complete his promise, Jodee Kulp from www.betterendings.org did her best to honor his graphic vision. YOU ARE MISSED

John and his Mother, Jorain Morgan Patronie

TABLE OF CONTENTS

ACKNOWLEDGMENTS ix

AUTHOR'S NOTE xi

1) CHRISTINE MEETS ROBERT 1

2) ELIZABETH'S BIRTHDAY.. 5

3) JAYNE AVE, PATCHOGUE, NEW YORK 13

4) ELIZABETH COMES TO JAYNE AVENUE...........................17

5) ELIZABETH SETTLES IN AND CHRISTINE DRIFTS AWAY......31

6) CHRISTINE ATTEMPTS SOBRIETY 35

7) A CHANCE ENCOUNTER AND ADOPTION SURRENDER 45

8) WHAT IS FETAL ALCOHOL SYNDROME? 59

9) STICKY FINGERS 65

10) THE WEDDING 71

11) CPS THREATS AND NIGHT TIME ADVENTURES................79

12) ADOPTION DAY 85

13) IMAGINARY FRIENDS 91

14) AN FAS EDUCATION FOR RICKY'S UNCLE 93

15) LAST YEAR AT ST. CHARLES EARLY

INTERVENTION PROGRAM 97

16) CHANEL'S NEW SCHOOL 101

17) HERE WE GO AGAIN-BABY REANNA 113

18) A TRAUMATIC EVENT IN CHANEL'S LIFE...................... 131

19) THE TORRES FAMILY MOVES TO FLORIDA 141

20) MORE TROUBLE FOR CHANEL 163

21) MEETING TRENT 181

22) CHANEL'S NEW CAREER 205

23) THE SEARCH IS ON 219

24) CHANEL'S RISE TO FAME 235

25) CHANEL MEETS ROBERT... 255

FINAL NOTES.. 265

CHANEL'S FINAL LETTER TO CHRISTINE 268

DO YOU NEED A MOTIVATIONAL SPEAKER....................... 271

ACKNOWLEGEMENTS

Chanel and I would like to express our utmost gratitude to Jodee Kulp from Better Endings, New Beginnings, for her invaluable assistance, support, guidance and patience. Without her knowledge and professional insight, this book would not have been possible. We share the same passion of educating as many people as possible on fetal alcohol syndrome. We encourage you to read all of Jodee and Liz Kulp's books.

We would also like to gratefully acknowledge Linda Dessau and Sharon Eaton for their help and time providing necessary feedback and editing.

Most of all we would like to thank Armando—husband and father—who has helped us along the way continuously urging us to write this book. Chanel and I would not have been able to complete this one year project, without him. Armando has given us heart whelming full support in making this educational project possible. We would both like to thank him from the bottom of our hearts for his tremendous help around the house. He has taken over primary responsibility of the endless household tasks: cooking, cleaning, laundry, helping with homework, grocery shopping, organizing the many doctor and ER visits for the children and even serving us meals right at our desk as we worked on our book. Never once complaining.

Finally and equally as important as all of the above, we want to thank Robert F. H. and Sue for their support and for providing us with valuable information that has contributed to this educational project.

AUTHOR'S NOTE

Parenting Chanel (who you will meet first as "Elizabeth") was one of the biggest challenges I have ever had to face and in return she has rewarded me with excitement, challenges, bewilderment and love.

Both Chanel and I have thoroughly researched the information about her birth mother Christine. Using both primary and secondary sources, friends and family of Christine's have provided us with a glimpse into the person she was. We also referenced documentation and letters written by Christine as well as a 40-minute conversation she and I had back in January of 1992. We have pieced all this together into what you will read in the first two chapters.

The remainder of the book is based on 22 years worth of my schedule books, with diary like entries to record the details of our lives.

To maintain privacy, some of the names have been changed.

CHAPTER ONE:

CHRISTINE MEETS ROBERT

C hristine was a relatively pretty 36 year old woman, with a fair complexion, and average height (5 ft. 3 in.) and weight. Her short, dark brown, wavy hair crowned her face subsiding just below her ears. She was most comfortable wearing jeans with a plain top and almost never adorned herself with makeup or jewelry. When she was sober, Christine was a determined, frank, fun, smart, loving and somewhat reasonable lady, add charming, flirtatious and alluring to that list. But when she was drunk, she transformed into a combative, disagreeable character that some-times spewed profanity out like hot lava from a volcano. The sad thing was, Christine was drunk more than she was sober.

Christine's parents lived in Florida and there was little com-munication between them. She was an only child with no siblings to confide in. She had only one girlfriend at this time, her drink-ing buddy, Cheryl.

Christine had given birth to one child prior to 1989. Her name was Susan. Susan moved up north to live with her father when she was nine, due to the unstable life style Christine was drawn to.

Robert came into Christine's life after meeting her at a house party one night sometime in the middle of 1988. He was invited to the party by his friend Tom. Christine was off in a distant corner with Cheryl, as they both sipped beer from a can. The moment Christine caught the attention of Robert; she

began to flirt with him incessantly, meandering her way closer to where he was standing. Robert was a handsome, strong looking, thirty-six-year-old man, standing about six feet tall and weighing slightly over 200 pounds. He was immediately drawn to Christine's side. "She was fun and funny; she made me laugh a lot" Robert told me. They both had a few beers before he offered to take her home, dropping her off at a "half-way-house" where she lived with other girls. They hit it off immediately and started seeing each other several times a week. Eventually they moved in together, sharing a sparsely-furnished motel room in BayShore, New York, utilizing a portable single burner cook-top for heating up their meals. A television and radio rested on the dresser top, Christine had no interest in either. "She certainly wasn't one to keep the place clean," Robert told me. "Dirty dishes were usually piled up on the dresser, the bed was rarely made, and several loads of laundry bags lay on the floor." Robert did his best to keep the room clean.

During the time Christine lived with Robert, she was able to secure a job in Brentwood, working in a textile factory. But she was unable to maintain the rigorous hours due to a back injury from a car accident she had a few years back when she was 19 years old. She had undergone four back surgeries to help relieve the unbearable pain that would radiate up into her spine. Sometimes her late night drinking episodes prevented her from showing up to work on time.

On the first of each month, Christine religiously waited for the mailman to deliver her welfare check. She used it to buy cigarettes and beer, any beer, whatever was on sale that day.

"Christine was very controlling, especially when she was drunk. If she got mad, she threw things at me, whatever she could get her hands on," Robert confided. "One time she left and didn't come back for three days." I was so worried about her, I was about to call the missing persons hot-line number, when she showed up at the hotel room drunk. I thought she could have been raped or killed! She was completely oblivious to my concerns and acted as though it was perfectly normal to take off for three days without telling me where she was. She later told me she stayed with several men (during that time)."

Robert stated that Christine's need to dominate whoever was with her was the reason he finally had enough and left after ten months.

Several months later Robert found some letters on top of his dresser from Christine, informing him that she was pregnant. Robert reflected back on all the times she left for several days spending time with several different men. How could she be sure this was his baby? Robert never responded to the letters and lost contact with Christine.

Sometime after this, Christine moved to Islip, New York with Harry and his two cats. Harry was 29 years older than Christine. Their apartment was a fairly decent place, with all the basic necessities. They were married sometime in 1990, after Elizabeth was born.

CHAPTER TWO:

ELIZABETH'S BIRTHDAY

December 31, 1989 was a chilly Sunday afternoon, about 35 degrees with a lingering overcast of rain mixed with a gently falling snow. Christine already drank several beers and her plan was to drink her pain away right into the New Year. Lord knows she has tried to stop drinking but as she told me later, "It's in my DNA and part of my chemical makeup."

"Stop! STOP! Harry, LEAVE ME ALONE! I just want one more, just one, Harry! I need a BEER. Get the HELL away from me. She shouted at Harry. The baby is fine. "I can feel it kicking inside me."

Harry thought he was helping Christine, but it made her very upset when he tried to stop her from drinking. '*Why stop now?*' she thought. She was already at least 35 weeks pregnant. (There was no way Christine knew for sure how far along she was-she didn't have any prenatal care.) She naively believed that if the baby was kicking, everything was okay.

Her labor began earlier this morning, and after medicating herself with another beer, she wasn't feeling much pain. Beer was her escape from this mess of a life she had gotten herself into. And now, she was about to bring someone else into her tangled up mess. A baby, an innocent little baby!

"Christine!! CHRISTINE!!! C'mon let's go. You're about to have a baby! Harry continued to yell and shout at Christine, as she hit him again and again, but Harry wasn't giving up. Christine continued to badger him and throw things at him, all while he wrestled a half-empty can of beer out of her hand and tried to help her into the car. Christine grabbed whatever she could get her hands on and tossed it at him. With the strength of a seasoned baseball pitcher, she was tossing things across the room, missing her intended target, Harry. She continued to fight him during one of her drunken tirades, laced with unimaginable profanity. But the pain was getting stronger and gaining more control over her, finally Harry was able to get her into the car. He sped off to Southside Hospital in BayShore. Christine screamed for help from the back seat while yelling out profanities intermittently with explosive cries for help. She could hear the tires screeching, and she felt every little bump in the road that would exacerbate her pain. As they entered the ER, Christine was quickly placed in a wheelchair and rushed off to the delivery room. There was no time for prepping. The fetal monitor was quickly set up as Christine forcefully started to push. Doctors urged her not to push "God damn it!" she screamed, "I can't stop, the baby is coming."

The doctors once again admonished Christine to STOP PUSH-ING, the baby was breech. One of the doctors instructed the nurse to restrain Christine's wrists to the side of the delivery table as he attempted to manually turn the baby into the birthing position.

"Okay," he told Christine, "it's time to push, PUUUUUUSH! Go ahead, Christine, PUSH!"

But just as Christine began to push again, the baby slipped back into breech position. The doctors gagged as they took turns delivering this tiny little life. The amniotic fluid was pungent and foul smelling. Fumes of rotten alcohol filled the cold and brightly lit room.

The time of birth 3:42 p.m., New Year's Eve, December 31, 1989, as the nurse yelled out the details so they could be recorded: "Apgar 9/9, breech presentation by vaginal delivery, no prenatal care. Mother has alcohol on her breath. Baby was suctioned and intubated times two for cleaning up her airway. Post extubation, baby will go to the special care nursery for close monitoring."

Christine heard the hustling and bustling of the nurses as they surrounded the baby and she recalled yelling out, "What is it doctor? What is it? "A boy, a girl?" As she slurred out words she wished for yet another beer, silently vowing, "JUST ONE MORE!! I promise to stop after this last one."

Reflections of a saying I once read:

Your beliefs become your thoughts. Your thoughts become your words. Your words become your actions. Your actions become your habits. Your habits become your values. Your values become your destiny.

Shortly after giving birth and still disoriented, Christine felt and sounded like a drunken sailor. Some of the hustle and bustle from the nurses calmed, and as the baby stabilized the neonatal specialist was ready to extubate her. The very loud shrills of the newborn baby's cries begin to fill the nursery, except this didn't sound like a normal cry. It was loud, so very loud. Christine feared the large overhead bright fluorescent light would shatter to bits and rain down on her as her legs were still up in the lithotomy position and her feet strapped into the stirrups. All while her hands were still restrained to the side of the delivery table. It was at this moment when it dawned on Christine that something was wrong; this baby was struggling for a breath, for life, for a chance! "What have I done? DAMN, what have I done?"

Christine only got a brief look at this tiny 4 lb., 2 oz. baby girl before she was whisked away to the special care nursery. She looked so very delicate with her very little fingers and eyes, tiny head and somewhat larger than usual ears. Christine finally dozed off into a drunken state of disbelief.

"I have to think of a name fit for a little princess, what about …..Elizabeth!" Christine paused, and then repeated "Elizabeth! Hmmmmm, that's it, I'm going to call her E-L-I-Z-Z-Z-A-B-E-T-H," as she slowly stretched out the name nodding her head with approval. "Today my baby is two days old, I have somewhat sobered up." Christine thought to herself. Her gathered thoughts were fleeting from one to the next as she reflected on the past two days. The guilt and shame of giving birth to a baby disabled by her own selfish alcohol use consumed her every thought. Her baby had been bathing in amniotic fluid laced with ethanol. The nurses remained distant toward her. She could hear them whis-

---

DISCHARGE SUMMARY:

GIRL CHILD
#8853533
M.D./F.   M.D.

ADMITTED: 12/31/89
DISCHARGED: 1/2▓/90

HISTORY: This is a 4 lb. 2 oz. female, born at Southside Hospital 12/31/89 at 3:42 pm., breech presentation by vaginal delivery, no prenatal care. Mother has alcohol on breath. Infant has an Apgar 9/9, meconium stained amniotic fluid, covered with thick meconium skin, nails and umbilical cord. She was suctioned and intubated times two for cleaning up her airway and then transferred to the Special Care Nursery.

PHYSICAL EXAMINATION: Initial physical examination, temperature 96 rectally; pulse 168; respiratory rate of 68; dip stix 90; color pink, good peripheral circulation, breathing comfortably. Chest by auscultation and percussion is clear bilaterally, good breath sounds. Heart is regular rate in rhythm without murmur, gallop or rub. The examination of the abdomen revealed soft, nontender abdomen, bowel sounds present and active, no masses, no hepatosplenomegaly, peripheral pulses equal in intensity in legs and arms. The examination of the head, ears, eyes, nose and throat revealed anterior fontanel open and flat, bilateral red reflex, pupils were equally round and reactive to light and accommodation. All limbs moving symmetrically, bruises prominent on buttocks, negative for CHD, spinal cord is closed, normal, slightly diminished muscle tonicity and strength. Baby is crying, sucking and active.

LABORATORY DATA: The complete blood count revealed a white blood count of 15.4, hemoglobin and hematocrit 14.3/42.6, platelet count 341,000, sodium 137, potassium 4.4, chloride 102, CO2 23, blood, urea and nitrogen 2, glucose 177, calcium 9. The neurological status was improved. The rapid plasma reagin test was negative. Mother's is O-negative. Cord blood is A-positive, direct Coombs negative. Urine toxicology positive only for alcohol. The complete blood count revealed a white blood count of 9.2, hemoglobin and hematocrit 14.8/45.4, 651 platelet count, 69 lymphs, 6 monos, 21 granulocytes, 4 eos. Head sonogram showed no evidence of intracranial hemorrhage or ventricular dilatation. The electrocardiogram on admission, which was done because of heart murmur suspected, sinus tachycardia rate of ventricular predominance. The chest X-ray, on admission to the hospital: normal heart size and pulmonary blood flow.

HOSPITAL COURSE: Infant was placed in an Isolette and connected to cardiac monitor. Peripheral line was inserted. Urine was sent for toxicology, CBC with lytes and assessment at that time, was 35 week gestation with microcephalic baby. Alcohol was detected in cord blood, 275. The neurological status improved, was actively sucking, grasp and Moro slightly diminished as well as muscle tone. Glucose infusion was subsequently continued.

DISCHARGE SUMMARY:

OMG, This is Elizabeth!!!

GIRL CHILD
#8853533
PAGE 2

Blood cultures were taken and negative. Blood alcohol was 275 mg per dl. The patient was seen in consultation with Dr. McCoyle, who recommended observation during regular pediatric care and cardiac re-evaluation in three months if murmur persists. He said a small patent ductus arteriosus cannot be excluded at this time. The patient did well during the hospitalization, was felt to be microcephalic, but gained weight. The neurological status improved. Systolic murmur was noted on the 22nd, when cardiology consult was called. There were no signs of cyanosis or hypoxia in the child. On the day of discharge the baby is 33 days old. The physical examination is essentially within normal limits except for the microcephalic head and systolic heart murmur, probably functional. Plan is to followup with Dr. Siddiq in two weeks and make appointment with the development center and to re-evaluate cardiac status in three months.

The Child Protective Services was contacted and felt baby could go home for followup.

CONDITION ON DISCHARGE: Satisfactory

FOLLOWUP: Office

FINAL DIAGNOSIS: NEWBORN, PRE-TERM AT THIRTY FIVE WEEKS TO MOTHER WITH ALCOHOL INTOXICATION

SW:ATM:jm
D 1/24/90
T 2/3/90

NMAN. M.D. /
F. S   M.D.

pering in the hall, "How negligent, cruel, irresponsible, heartless and selfish!" Christine wasn't sure if this was just her hallucinatory guilt or did she actually hear the nurses say these awful things, did she really do this to her baby?

She never did go for prenatal care, perhaps she was afraid the doctor would try to stop her selfish pastime with lectures and educational pamphlets, as well as an explanation on the potential consequences of drinking any alcoholic beverages while pregnant. It's probable even a doctor's admonishments could not have stopped her from drinking. Michael, her first husband, Robert her live-in boyfriend and Harry, who was her boyfriend at the time of the birth, and eventually became her second husband; none of them were successful at getting Christine to maintain sobriety.

Christine came from a long family history of alcoholics. Her mother, Bridget Josephine; father, Walter Joseph Jr.; and her grandfather, Walter Joseph Sr.; were all alcoholics, as well as other family members. Her alcoholic legacy followed her all the way from Ireland, where her grandparents emigrated in the 1920's. She had been predisposed to alcoholism, Christine would later proclaim to me. She often wondered if her mother was inebriated 37 years ago on June 21, 1952, while giving birth to her.

January 3, 1990 was Christine's discharge day. The baby was three days old and still struggling. The doctors had detected a heart murmur. Wires had been attached to her tiny little chest, and it was difficult for Christine to hold her. Elizabeth cried relentlessly, it was impossible to console or comfort her.

As Christine was packing her belongings for discharge, two women neatly dressed in professional attire approached her. "Please sit down for a moment, we'd like to talk to you," one of them said.

"Hello, Christine, my name is Mrs. Craven and this is Mrs. Taylor. I work with Child Protective Services and Mrs. Taylor is a social worker. We are here because we received a report that your baby's blood alcohol level was 274 mg/dl at delivery time." (In most states 100 mg/dl or above for an *adult* represents the threshold concentration above which a person is legally intoxicated when operating a motor vehicle.) "We are concerned about the health and well being of your newborn baby girl after discharge. She will need to remain here at the hospital for a few more weeks for observation. In the meantime, I will schedule home visits at your residence to determine if it is suitable for a baby. If we find it is not, then we will ask you to sign a voluntary surrender form and the baby will go into foster care temporarily until you complete drug and alcohol rehab. We also have a criteria list for you to fulfill in order for your baby to come live with you. If you refuse to sign the voluntary surrender papers, then we will have no other choice but to get a court ordered surrender."

The social worker then handed the paperwork to Christine for her to sign.

> "I Christine_____, hereby voluntarily surrender my baby girl to CPS temporarily until I am able to fulfill my obligations listed below."

Tears streamed from her cheeks, and her hand shook uncontrollably as she signed the papers.

CHAPTER THREE

JAYNE AVE, PATCHOGUE, NEW YORK

Torres home is on the left.

The village of Patchogue, population 11,060, was named after the Native American Patchogue Indian Tribe. The village is 2.5 square miles and approximately 60 miles east of Manhattan, New York. Patchogue is a small, well maintained town with lots of small specialty boutiques, mom and pop stores, good schools and small family churches. It is a very family-friendly community, which the Torres family fell in love with. At 71 East Main

Street, there is a beautiful theater for the performing arts that was completely restored in the late 1990's, and seats 1,166. The Patchogue library was like a second home to our family. Wonderful restaurants line Main Street and in the summer, every Saturday night the entire street was closed off to traffic for family fun, food, games and shopping. The tantalizing aromas from the steaming hot food venders spread through the air, magically drawing village residents to the festivities.

My parents, Willis and Rosina Morgan, were the owners of the Bellport Casino in Bellport, slightly east of Patchogue, for approximately 20 years. The Morgan family was pretty well known to Long Islanders. I vowed to stay close to my roots, so it was no surprise that after I married Armando Torres, I remained on Long Island.

The Torres family moved to 63 Jayne Avenue, only two blocks from Main Street, at the end of February, 1974. At this time we were a family of four; Armando (my husband), Sondra (me) and our two daughters, Trudy and Alexa. The house was an old, three story, light gray, Victorian home with a turret to the left that wrapped around to the front.

The neighborhood was surrounded by big oak trees. In the springtime, beautiful hot pink Azalea florets dotted the front and back yard. Huge reddish/pink Rhododendron bushes filled the yards on both the north and south side of our home. There was one soft pink flowering crab apple tree nestled right between our house and Gail's (our good friend and next-door neighbor). The summers were hot and humid and the children almost always cooled down under a running sprinkler in the mid afternoon.

Autumn on Long Island was the season for sweaters, warm cocoa and playing in Dad's neat pile of leaves. The glorious foliage turned from green to a kaleidoscope of reds, oranges, yellows and different shades of purple.

The transition from autumn to winter was always exciting because it reminded us that our favorite holiday was right around the corner. The naked trees and bushes were now void of bright pretty color. A thin blanket of soft white snow covered the tops of all the trees and bushes. Each of Long Island's four seasons always represented a new beginning.

The roots from the 100 year old large oak trees pushed their way above the uneven sidewalk on either side of Jayne Avenue; from Oak Street and beyond Roe Boulevard, almost to Sunrise Highway.

Our family knew just about everyone on Jayne Avenue. We were like one big happy family. There were lots of neighborhood children for our kids to play with, and our house was where most of the kids hung out. I didn't mind; as a matter-of-fact I encouraged it. This way, I always knew where my children were and who they were with.

Our home was filled with laughter, friends, neighbors, children, and foster children; back yard BBQ's, a collection of tricycles and lots of other outdoor toys were strewn about the yard. Of course there were the occasional sibling rivalry, time outs, and disappointed teens unhappy about the curfew; and yes, there were tears, teen arguments, Mom and Dad arguments, hugs, sadness, happiness, joy, family commitment and most of all LOVE.

It was always someone's birthday party, so forget about dieting. Armando did most of the cooking, while I did all of the baking. His cooking always piqued the interest of our neighbors, especially Gail, who Armando loved to share his favorite Puerto Rican foods with.

Most of our neighbors were close friends. We all watched out for each other's children. Miriam was always baking something yummy, Gail was ready to go yard sale shopping and Debbie and I could chat for hours and never get tired. Eileen was my craft buddy and always ready to baby sit. Cathy and John would come over to play an occasional card game that lasted until the wee hours of the morning.

CHAPTER FOUR

ELIZABETH COMES TO JAYNE AVENUE

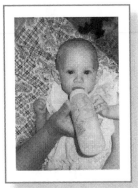

On January 22, 1990, a foster care placement worker called me to ask if I would take in baby Elizabeth. At first I turned him down, explaining to him that I had just taken in an 11- month old a few weeks ago with spina bifida and didn't know if it would be too much on my family. When I asked him what her diagnosis was he replied, "I know she was born to an alcoholic mother. It says here on the paper, probable diagnosis: fetal alcohol syndrome." I had no clue what that was. I asked if I could research that and get back to him.

We didn't have a computer, so off to the Patchogue Library I went to find out about fetal alcohol syndrome. There wasn't very much information on it and most of what I read said that this was a birth defect that is 100% preventable just by maintaining complete abstinence from consuming alcoholic beverages while pregnant. I also read that babies with fetal alcohol syndrome cry a lot and that they're hard to console.

The very next day before I had a chance to call the foster care placement desk, my phone rang, "Hello, Mrs. Torres, this is Bob from the foster care unit. So, have you thought about taking in baby Elizabeth?"

"Yes, after talking things over with my husband Armando, we have decided to give it a try. When will she come to us?"

Bob replied, "Elizabeth could come to you by tomorrow morning."

Sondra and Armando Torres

It was January 24, 1990, the night was chilly. I could hear a gentle wind blowing through the trees as I tossed and turned trying to sleep, peeking up at the clock only to find out it was five minutes since the last time I looked. I was excited and nervous all at the same time. My thoughts were running wild. "Are we doing the right thing? Can we handle two special needs babies at the same time?"

On Wednesday, January 24, 1990 at 9:30 a.m., a mix of rain and snow was now falling, and the wind continued to gently blow the naked tree branches back and forth. The temperature outside was about 40 degrees. After fostering children without birth anomalies for over 13 years, we were about to get our second baby with special needs, all within a few weeks. I paced the floor, peeking out the window every time a car passed, wondering if this was my special delivery.

Finally, a white van pulled into our driveway, I could see two women removing a small box-like carrier covered with a brightly-colored cloth from the back seat. I ran to the door with anticipation as my foster baby Tiffany lay quietly in her playpen.

"Hello," I quietly said to the women at the door, right at that moment my excitement could no longer be contained, "How are you? I can't wait to see her, come on in and get out of the cold. Let me see this little baby." I don't remember their names but I do remember one was a CPS (Child Protective Service) worker and the other was a public health nurse. The nurse placed the baby and the carrier on my sofa and proceeded to uncover her. My heart was racing, I could hardly wait to see this little one. "There, THERE she is!! Oh my God, she's very tiny, Oh wow, WOW! Oh my God!" At first, I was afraid to pick her up, but it didn't take long before I gave it a try. The nurse took baby Elizabeth out of her carrier and put her in my arms. Elizabeth was crying, so I attempted to comfort her. The nurse showed me how to hold the baby close to my body. Yet, no matter what position I placed the baby in, it just didn't seem to calm her. The two women gave me some paper work, a few diapers and formula then reminded me to make an appointment with the pediatrician in one week. They said their good byes and off they went, leaving me with a screaming new born baby.

Hours passed and all my attempts to calm baby Elizabeth had been futile. I placed her in a baby swing and BINGO, it calmed her. I raced over to care for baby Tiffany, but just as I picked her up, Elizabeth's cries were loud and furious once again. I quickly changed Tiffany's diaper and fed her, all while Elizabeth screamed on and off.

It was nearing 3:30 p.m., school was about to end for three of my older daughters. One by one, they ran into the house with great anticipation to see the new baby. They each took turns holding her tiny little body, fighting over who would hold her next. Jessica seemed to light up when it was her turn. Despite Elizabeth's crying, she still didn't part with her easily when it was time to put Elizabeth down for a quiet nap.

It was difficult to feed Elizabeth. Not only did she have some issues with sucking on a nipple but she cried so often and furiously that it was challenging and at times an impossible task. Most babies revel in warm, close physical contact with their care giver, but not this munchkin. I continued to attempt different calming techniques to comfort her, holding her close to my body, stroking her little head and arms, as well as rocking her slowly while sitting in my favorite chair. However, none of my efforts to calm her worked. What do you do when your baby will not stop crying? I carried her in a football hold. I gently bounced her on a ball. I carried her in a sling and massaged her tummy. I gave her three lavender baths, hoping the warm water would soothe her. It did stop the crying for a minute or two. I even tried driving with her in the car. Everyone said that would help, but in fact it aggravated her even more.

By 4:00 p.m. I was so exhausted; all I wanted was some quiet time. Armando was about to arrive home from work, Tiffany needed attention, the other kids wanted help with home-work and I was five loads of laundry behind. The door-bell and phone were ringing; the dog was barking and Elizabeth continued to exercise her lungs to the max.

Thirteen days later, On February 5, 1990 a social worker called to inform me that Elizabeth would have her first home visit with her mother Christine and her live in boyfriend, Harry. I was told that a transportation worker would pick Elizabeth up at 11:15 a.m. the following day. I was SOOO looking forward to this break.

On February 6, 1990, sure enough, a white van pulled up exactly at 11:15 a.m. as promised. As the driver approached the front door I was frantically gathering all the necessary things to put into Elizabeth's baby bag, which was a beautiful and unique bag that was hand crafted by one of my friends. It was quilted out of fabric and adorned with large cabbage roses. I rushed to complete this task as Elizabeth's cries were becoming more and more frantic. I gladly handed her over to the driver but just as I was about to quickly shut the door and begin my four-and-half-hour respite break from the constant crying, the driver turned toward me and said, "This is your chance to take a break, relax and get some rest while you have the chance."

"No break for me," I told her, "I still have to catch up on laundry, take care of little Tiffany, make several phone calls, do some paper-work and attend a parent/teacher meeting at 12:00 p.m." 3:30 p.m. came so quickly that for a moment I thought the clock was broken. Elizabeth returned just as she left-crying. Now I was convinced something must be wrong with baby Elizabeth, so I made an appointment for her to see Dr. Ost at the Brookhaven Health Center in town.

She now weighed 6 lbs and was 19 inches long. Dr. Ost explained to me that while Elizabeth's ethanol withdrawals had past, I must remember that Elizabeth was not an ordinary baby with ordinary problems. She went on to explain, "There was a time we thought the placenta protected babies from alcohol, but we now know that's not true. Elizabeth is a recovering alcoholic and might still crave alcohol. This will pass with love, nurturing and patience from you and your family."

Relieved to know Elizabeth was fine, I left the doctor's office thinking, "I can do this! I can do this! I can do this!"

On February 22, 1990, Elizabeth was scheduled to have the second home visit with her mother. The transportation service arrived just as promised at 1:30 p.m. Once again I was more than happy to hand over the baby as her cries seemed to be getting louder and more intense, if that's even possible. These home visits continued on a consistent weekly basis. I would bathe her in a nice warm lavender bath, dry her off and then massage her with my favorite Johnson & Johnson baby lotion. Each week she wore a brand new dress embellished with lace, beading and puckering, with a pair of fancy socks and patent leather Mary Jane shoes to complete the look. I would pack her special baby bag with all her necessities plus a few toys, and off she went. I often wondered what the transportation driver did to drown out the screeching cries on the 20-minute drive from Patchogue to Islip.

Each time Elizabeth returned from her home visit, the Johnson & Johnson new baby smell was replaced with an odor of stale cigarette smoke, her pretty new dress was filthy, and her fingernails had black something or other caked under the nail beds. Her hair was a mess and she had cat hair all over her. I reported my concerns to the social worker; particularly that Elizabeth was breathing in second hand smoke. I waited to see improvement, but it never came.

I had no idea a baby could cry almost non-stop for so many consecutive weeks. I thought she was testing my patience. As a nurse, I had been working the overnight shift from 11:00 p.m. to 7:00 a.m. on the weekends. I paid Alexa, my 17 year-old daughter, to hold and calm baby Elizabeth while I worked. I never knew how Armando could sleep right through her cries. Each weekend morning at 7:30 a.m. as I arrived home through the back door of the kitchen, Alexa was always ready to give me her report, "Elizabeth cried almost all night. No matter what I did to comfort her, nothing seemed to work." I assured Alexa we could not give up on Elizabeth. I was *SURE* in ten years the cries would stop.

The home visits continued on weekly basis, usually on a Tuesday or Thursday. On June 24, 1990, again I was happy to hand Elizabeth over to the transportation driver for my four-hour break, but on this day I didn't get a break. The social worker called and said she was concerned about leaving Elizabeth with her mother because Christine sounded drunk on the phone. The visit was canceled. Somehow I wasn't very upset about the canceled visit. I didn't want Elizabeth with someone who would not be able to take care of herself, let alone a non-stop screaming baby.

Although the weekly visits with her birth mom continued, I found myself more and more reluctant to hand Elizabeth over to the transportation driver. I wasn't sure what was happening, I was experiencing strange feelings inside me, not wanting to part with this baby even if it was only for four hours. What was happening? I had been trying not to bond with her. I'd been told by the case worker that the plan for Elizabeth was to return her home with her mother, though a long list of requirements had to be fulfilled before this could happen. Christine had already started her first attempt at alcohol rehabilitation at the Charles K. Post Addiction Treatment Center. Harry had an acceptable income and they had a fairly decent apartment. So as soon as the other tasks were completed, Elizabeth would be returned to her mother.

When the case worker told me this, I felt very sad and wanted to fall to the ground. It is at this moment I realize, "OH MY GOD! I LOVE ELIZABETH!" I began thinking God awful thoughts, "I hope Elizabeth's mother Christine will get drunk and not finish her rehab."

On June 6, 1990, at 2:30 in the afternoon, (Elizabeth was a little more than six months old) I was excited because Elizabeth would be evaluated at St. Charles hospital. This evaluation would get her started with the home-based early intervention program provided by St. Charles. Perhaps with therapy and time we could comfort this little one. Elizabeth's evaluation was completed and she soon started home-based early intervention, just like Tiffany. If I thought our home was busy before, it was about to get a whole lot busier.

Christine often sent notes home in the baby bag, when I checked the bag on June 8, 1990, I found this note:

> *Dear Sondra*   *6/8/90*
> *Thank you for taking such good care of Elizabeth. You have done a great job in helping her develop. Each time I see her, I see a great deal of improvement.*
> *Once again,*   *thank you,*   *Chris*

July 15, 1990 was a very important day for my family, as we gathered for a monumental event, Elizabeth's baptism at St. Joseph's Catholic Church in East Patchogue. Trudy my first born daughter was about to become Elizabeth's God Mother. Surprisingly Elizabeth didn't cry very much during the ceremony though the silence was short lived. As family, friends, neighbors and co-workers congregated for a back-yard party and BBQ to celebrate this special day, the loud boom box radio over-powered Elizabeth's cries as each one of my guests announced they knew exactly how to calm a crying baby. Elizabeth was passed around from friend

Elizabeth about to
get baptized

to friend to have a chance, but not one was able to calm her for more than 5-10 minutes at a time before the screeching cries resumed.

On Thursday, July 29, 1990, we had a visit from Barbara, our new case worker. As I greeted her at the front door with Elizabeth in my arms, I began to say "Hello Barbara, how nice to meet you" What happens next just absolutely crushed me!!

Barbara reached out to shake my hand and proceeded to say "Oh wow! They didn't tell me you have a baby with FAS, they told me your baby has spina bifida."

I wanted to bend down and scoop my heart up off the floor. Instead, I found the strength to ask, "If they didn't tell you I had a baby with FAS, then, *HOW* did you know?"

She replied: "Oh my dear, I have worked with FAS kids for a long time. I can spot them a mile away."

I invited her in and introduced her to my older daughter's and then to our beautiful foster daughters Tiffany and Elizabeth. Barbara and I retreated to the kitchen for a private talk, where she asked me, "How did you get two foster children under the age of two?"

"Well, Tiffany came to us mid-December, and then a few weeks later a placement worker called and asked if I would take Elizabeth, so we now have two foster children that we adore!" I happily replied.

Barbara got up from her seat with a puzzled look, said her good-bye's and left. The very next day she called me to say she wanted to see me on Monday, ALONE! She sounded serious, but

I didn't ask what she wanted to talk to me about for fear of opening up a can of worms. I just wasn't in the mood for a lecture at this time.

After a home visit on August 3, 1990, I found another note:

Dear Sondra   *8, 3. 1990*

Thank you for the beautiful pictures, they are real nice.

You are doing a real nice job with Elizabeth. Right now Chris is holding her on her lap, watching "Sesame Street" on T.V. She seems to be fascinated with it.

Chris' mother and dad were up from Fla. They were surprised to see "Lizzy" and fell in love with her.

Sondra, as an afterthought, could you please send the negatives of the pictures you sent? We want to send the pictures to Chris' mother. Thank You.   Will close for now

Christine & Harry

It was Monday, August 6, 1990, the day of my meeting with the case worker, Barbara. She arrived at 2:00 p.m., as planned, and was escorted into the kitchen by one of my older daughters. Soon after entering the kitchen she turned to my girls and in an authoritative voice she told them not to disturb us, then continued to instruct my girls to answer the phone if it rang. This made me really nervous. I still had *NO* idea why she was here to see me;

I knew it must be urgent since she was demanding privacy in such a dominant tone.

As I nervously sat at my kitchen table, I couldn't believe what Barbara just told me, I wanted to cry, but I didn't because of what a foster mom friend once told me, "Don't ever let the case workers see you cry, or they will see you as weak" hmmmmm not sure what to make of this, I WAS WEAK! I wanted to CRY!! Oh my God! I couldn't believe what Barbara had just asked me!

"Sondra I'm not sure if you know this, but you're not allowed to have two foster children under the age of two, so I will have to remove one. It's in the policy book. So tell me-which one do you want me to take away?"

I respond "Ohhh, my God! Barbara I can't believe you're asking me this, it would be the same thing as if you asked me which of my older daughters would I part with, Trudy, Alexa, Jessica, Dana or Brendalyn!!!"

Barbara replied, "I will give you a few days to decide and I'll be calling you soon."

My ears, my head, chest, belly, feet, soul, heart, legs, hands and every cell in my body were all experiencing intractable pain. I couldn't think straight, I couldn't eat; I couldn't get those words out of my head. As the shock wore off, I got fired up and asked all my neighbors to write a letter stating how long they have known Armando and me and how well they thought we were taking care of our children and our foster children. I was thrilled that each neighbor returned a letter to me by the next morning.

August 10, 1990 at 10:a.m., the dreaded phone call arrived.

Barbara said that since I had not been able to make the choice of which baby to part with, she had made the choice for me, "I will take Tiffany."

Remembering what my friend told me about not crying in front of the case worker completely eluded me, I started crying uncontrollably, begging her not to take little Tiffany away from us. Barbara's attempts to console me were both fruitless and ambiguous.

After reading each one of the kind and earnestly supportive letters, I expeditiously mailed them off to Barbara's boss in Ronkonkoma, N.Y., and followed up with a phone call to him. This time I tried my best not to cry, but a few tears escaped. He listened to me for about 12 minutes with very few interruptions. I'm not sure if he ever received the letters, and I had no further contact with him. Barbara continued to make visits to our home on a regularly scheduled basis, but never mentioned the letters, my phone call to her boss, or removing Tiffany again. Tiffany stayed with the Torres Family!

CHAPTER FIVE:

ELIZABETH SETTLES IN AND CHRISTINE DRIFTS AWAY

M y sister, Brenda; my brother, Willis Morgan Jr.; my mother Rosina Morgan and other family members wanted to meet Elizabeth. With special written permission from Elizabeth's mom and her case worker, Barbara, on August 15, 1990, Elizabeth took her first plane ride to Florida for a six-day vacation.

Grandma, Rosina Morgan with Elizabeth

Back at home, Armando and other family members visited Tiffany as much as possible at the hospital. She was not able to make the visit to Florida since she had just undergone bilateral hip surgery at St. Charles Hospital in Port Jefferson.

My mother really enjoyed Elizabeth and each family member took turns holding her. They were amazed at how tiny she was

31

for her age. Elizabeth's cries were less frequent, but continued to be ear piercing when she did cry.

Aunt Brenda holds Elizabeth

Fall arrived a few weeks after returning to New York from Florida. Elizabeth's cries were less frequent; I finally realized how much I absolutely loved this rambunctious baby girl. When I was away from her I couldn't get her off my mind. She was now ten months old and still very tiny. I kept her in a baby pouch right next to my body as I did errands, cleaned the house and cared for little Tiffany.

Cousin John and Elizabeth

On October 4, 1990, as usual the transportation service came to take my little Elizabeth for her weekly home visit with Christine. I wasn't happy about handing her over. Darn, I wished I could've pretended she was sick so I could cancel the visit. But of course that didn't happen. As I handed "MY" baby over to this woman I started kissing Elizabeth over and over as if it would be the last time I would see her. Soon after shutting the door I found myself crying and pacing the floor back and forth. I couldn't take the wait!

Approximately one hour and ten minutes later I was still at the window as the white van pulled up into my driveway, much earlier than expected. The driver revealed that Christine had been very drunk and, Elizabeth's visit was canceled. I was so happy to hold her, hug her, kiss her and know she was back in a safe, loving environment.

Just a few days later on October 26, 1990, another home visit was canceled, this time because Christine was arguing very loudly with Harry. The neighbors called the police, who showed up just as Elizabeth was arriving in the white van. Visits were suspended for a few weeks. After several weeks of no visits, Christine called the case worker to set up another home visit for November 2, 1990 only to have it canceled because Christine was drunk AGAIN!! At this time Barbara (the case worker) determined that all home visits were canceled until further notice.

Elizabeth continued with home-based early intervention as I watched her progress unfold. Her special education teacher arrived at 9 a.m. every Monday, Wednesday and Friday with a bag full of new toys for Elizabeth to play and learn from. Although she was not meeting the usual milestones for a ten-month-old baby i.e.: crawling, improved hand-eye coordination, attempting to feed herself or sitting up without assistance, she was making some progress and beginning to smile more often. At this point she didn't recognize me as her main caregiver so she didn't mind being separated from me for an extended period of time.

The weekly home visits were reestablished once again but not for long. Christine was a no-show for an important meeting at the St. Charles Early Intervention Program in Port Jefferson. We were there for an evaluation that would allow Elizabeth to attend the pre-school rather than the home-based program. I knew she would benefit from the increase in frequency and intensity of these sessions from three days to five days a week. I was most happy about the socialization skills she would be exposed to. The principal of the program illuminated that the rate of learning and development was most rapid during the pre-school years, and this program would allow Elizabeth to reap maximum benefits. After careful evaluation, Elizabeth was accepted for the school-based program and was scheduled to start in one month.

On December 17, 1990, Elizabeth was picked up for a home visit but was quickly returned to me. Christine had been arrested after getting drunk and beating up Harry. Neighbors once again called police, who found Christine to be the aggressor. She was handcuffed and taken to jail in a patrol car.

Meanwhile, our first Christmas with Elizabeth was wonderful. On December 24, 1990, Christmas Eve, the Torres family all gathered at our Jayne Avenue home for fun, food, laughter, love and lots and lots of gifts. Christmas was our favorite time of year. I truly believed that no one did Christmas like the Torres family! Elizabeth sat in her walker and observed the merriment. At this point we had not heard from Christine since December 17th.

On New Year's Eve I sang happy birthday to my little princess. Our celebration was small, with just a few friends, neighbors and family to have birthday cake and help Elizabeth open up her gifts. We still hadn't heard a word from Christine. Not even a birthday card for Elizabeth's first birthday.

CHAPTER SIX:

CHRISTINE
ATTEMPTS SOBRIETY

After spending approximately one week incarcerated, Christine was released from jail. A couple weeks later her visitations with Elizabeth once again resumed and were fairly consistent, lasting about four hours with very few cancellations.

On January 31, 1991 I found this note in Elizabeth's baby bag after a home visit:

> *Dear Sondra,*
>
> *Elizabeth is beautiful! She is doing great. I am so glad to see her!*
>
> *We have a cat also and she is going after him calling cat-cat!*
>
> *I don't know if Barbara (the case worker) told you or not but, I am going into C. K. Post Tuesday. It's a three week program to help me with the alcohol prob-*

> *lem. I will never be "cured" but, I will be about to understand this problem. I am glad you and your family love Elizabeth and I thank you all for the love and care you are giving her. Barbara and I have spoken about the open adoption and I really believe I will do this. Once again I thank you.*
>
> *Love and all my best   Chris*

The C. K. Post facility holds 79 beds for inpatients and 29 beds for their community residential program. Therapists at the facility focus on the emotional and social reasons for addiction. After Christine graduated from the program sometime at the end of February with a good report of sobriety she was directed into a day program and was able to maintain a steady attendance.

Christine continued to live with Harry, who enabled her drinking by buying her beer when her welfare money ran out and often drinking alongside her. I truly believed that separating Christine from Harry would have been beneficial for her recovery.

Although I was happy Christine was making progress and moving forward toward her goal, it once again raised my fear of losing Elizabeth. At the foster care headquarters in Ronkonkoma, periodic meetings with a group of case workers and their supervisors that hardly knew Elizabeth, took place. Her fate was in their hands.

I loved her more than they could possibly imagine. I wanted to be able to protect her for the rest of her life from any harm that may come her way. I never knew what tomorrow would bring so all I could do was be prepared for the worst and pray for the best. Armando and I had been foster parents for a long time and knew that unpredictable things could happen at any time without warning.

In April 1991, I found this letter from Christine in Elizabeth's bag after a home visit:

Dear Sondra,

Elizabeth looks so good and you dress her so nice. I had to wear glasses as a child. I had a lazy left eye. I ended up having the muscles tightened twice.You are going to have a job trying to keep them on her.

I don't know if Barbara (the case worker) told you or not but, I'm trying very hard to stop drinking. I spent two months up at C.K. Post and now I am in a day program here in Bay Shore. I'll be in this program for about 6 mos. and then hopefully, I'll be able to enroll in nursing. I want to eventually work with handicap children. I always did but somewhere along the line I got messed up.

I can't begin to tell you how much your caring for Elizabeth has meant to me. I really am trying to get my life together and because of the great care and love you have given her I don't have to worry. I wish I could see her more and be more involved in her life. Thank you for everything and especially, for your note

Sincerely, Chris

On July 31, 1991, I found another note in Elizabeth's baby bag:

Dear Sondra   *July 31, 1991*

Just a short note to express my appreciation to you for sending me the beautiful pictures of Elizabeth. I can't begin to tell you how much I love them. She is doing beautiful and even took a few steps by herself. One of the guys at my school lent me a port-a crib for Elizabeth's visits, it comes in handy. She can play and talk on her phone I gave her nothing to eat but she seemed to be looking for her ice cream, she kept bringing me into the kitchen. She really is improving; I see it every time I see her. I look forward to her visits so much and once again I thank you for all the love and care you give her.

All my best to you and your family
Chris

I was informed by the case worker that Christine had requested to increase her visits with Elizabeth from four hours per visit to six hours, then possibly over-nights. I knew there was a strong possibility that she would be awarded this request, since Christine had

Elizabeth with her new glasses

completed a course of treatment at the Charles K. Post Addiction Center in Brentwood, New York.

Elizabeth and I had developed an unbelievable bond that had been growing subtly for some time. I feared the day would come when the case worker would call and inform us that Elizabeth must return to Christine. The Suffolk County Department of Social Services had been honest and open with me. They didn't lead me into any false hopes; I seemed to be able to do that all by myself without their assistance.

By now I had gathered up a ton of information on fetal alcohol syndrome from teachers, therapists and foster parents, as well

Elizabeth and birth mom, Christine

Elizabeth and Christine

as from my own observations and experiences with Elizabeth. I was beginning to understand it as I watched it unfold before me. Like all children, those with fetal alcohol syndrome need a supportive home environment with guidelines that are age appropriate; always allowing them to communicate openly without the fear of punishment. All children need to feel loved, but especially a child with fetal alcohol syndrome in order to decrease the behavioral issues that are likely to occur in later years. I saw for myself and learned that the best progress came when the home environment was quiet, stable and predictable, without loud arguments or disruptive behavior. This helps eliminate the child's feeling of being anomalous. Children with fetal alcohol syndrome who are raised in a home with clear boundaries, and who have been given simple, one-step instructions they can carry out with success, have a better chance of having reduced (not eliminated) behavioral problems later on. I have always believed in a firm yet loving discipline for all of my children. I show them that I will love them unconditionally through the good, bad and ugly. Some parents have set high expectations for their child with fetal alcohol syndrome, only to find out how frustrating it could be, for the child and for the parent, when the child is unable to fulfill these expectations due to their lower than average IQ or behavioral functional age.

On August 14, 1991, I received this note from Christine:

Dear Sondra,   *8/14/1991*

Just a short note to let you know how much I enjoyed Elizabeth today.

We took a walk up to Waldbaums to get bananas! She had a half of one. My girlfriend Betty came over and we went down to the beach. Elizabeth was in the water, she loves it. I rinsed her suit out because of the salt water. She is a treasure and I cherish every moment with her.

As far as the fevers go have they checked her ears?

> *Her sister Susan used to run high fevers until I had*
> *her tonsils out. Maybe that's it.*
> *Thank you again for the love and care you are giving*
> *her.*
>
> *Chris*

I knew the most important thing was to focus on making everyday a special day for Elizabeth and to enjoy every moment I had with her. I registered Elizabeth for story time at the Patchogue Library. This gave us "mommy and me" time to interact with each other as well as with other children in our neighborhood, without the normal disruptions experienced at home; the phone ringing, someone knocking at the door, requests for help from the other children, dogs barking, etc. Elizabeth was now 20 months old and didn't quite know what the story-teller was saying, but she loved sitting in my lap. It seemed to calm her and provide entertainment for a short time.

Christine continued to send notes home in Elizabeth's baby bag. They were all complimentary. This one came on September 26, 1991:

> *Dear Sondra,*   *9/26/1991*
> *Thank you for your letter. I enjoy getting them! Eliz-*
> *abeth is doing great and I had a ball playing with*
> *her. She loves the water and walked me out to the sink*
> *so I put her in. She had a peanut butter sandwich,*
> *some of her milk and ice water. She slept for about an*
> *hour. I love her so much and all I want is the best for*

> *her. I am hoping to start school soon. I want to go for nursing too!*
>
> *I am going to close now, Elizabeth fell outside today, I took her for a walk and she tripped going from the grass to the sidewalk   Thank you,   Chris*

As I was sitting next to Elizabeth while she slept in her crib, I whispered to her, "Sleep tight, little one. I love you so much." As I softly stroked her sweet smelling hair, I wondered what direction her life would take. She slept so peacefully in her crib, blissfully unaware of all the legal proceedings and discussions that were taking place about her in Ronkonkoma, I savored that precious moment.

I knew that Christine was at high risk for relapse. After all, this wasn't the first time she had attempted rehab. As long as she was living with Harry, the temptations and cravings were bound to resume.

I wanted so much for Elizabeth to spend the rest of her growing years with the Torres family. Each day I spent with her was a gift as I never knew what tomorrow would bring. How would I handle the news if the group of case workers and their supervisors decided Elizabeth should live with Christine?

Elizabeth and birth mom, Christine

I often thought about Christine and was unable to understand why she couldn't stop drinking for just the few months she carried Elizabeth. Wasn't she aware how harmful her drinking was to the growing fetus inside her? If she could go to C.K. Post and stop drinking for several months after she gave birth, why not during the pregnancy? If only she had, Elizabeth would not be a prisoner to fetal alcohol syndrome. I asked myself these questions over and over again. Questions I will never have an answer to.

Elizabeth's weekly visits with Christine continued throughout 1991, with very few cancellations by Christine. Towards the end of the year, her visits were extended from 9:00 a.m. until 5:30 p.m. This really concerned me. I often wondered if Christine refrained from drinking for the hours Elizabeth was with her. Elizabeth continued to return to me with the awful smell of stale cigarette smoke and covered in cat hair. Due to Christine having a few episodes of alcohol relapse, overnight visits were never granted.

Below are a few more notes I found in the baby bag during this time:

> *Dear Sondra,*
>
> *Thank you so much for your letter. My problem is getting the work I need through this program I am in now. Elizabeth is doing so well, I enjoy her visits so much. You dress her beautiful. Today we took pictures and she is a ham and sure knows a camera!*
>
> *I really want to go for the nursing!*
> *Where do you find the time?*

Do you have a cat? Elizabeth sure does love ours.
Barbara (the case worker) said she isn't adjusting
well to the glasses, my mom said she had a hard time
with me too.
Thanks once again   Chris

Dear Sondra

Just a quick note to let you know how big Eliza-
beth has gotten. Harry and I took her up to the South
Shore Mall to try to get an idea of what she would
like for Christmas. Does she need a winter coat? Please

give me some ideas as to what she can use. I'm send-
ing some things home with her. I hope you can use
them. Thanks for caring for her. What happened to her
hand, she keeps showing it to me
Thanks again   Chris
PS the dresses were Elizabeth's older sisters!
I got them from my mom's
Hope you can use them

The winter of 1991 was a cold one and Elizabeth loved to play in the snow. Together we made a rather large snow man with the typical carrot nose, large side by side buttons to form a smile and a top hat, making sure not to forget the scarf around his neck to keep him warm. Elizabeth made snow angels before we went in for hot chocolate with marshmallows. What a wonderful way to end the year.

CHAPTER SEVEN:

A CHANCE ENCOUNTER
AND ADOPTION SURRENDER

1992 started off with the famous NY cold wind that penetrated every fiber in my body. Whenever I took Elizabeth out for a doctor's appointment, I had to bundle her up three times over so her tiny little body stayed warm.

On this particular day in January the wind was blistering; my eyes welled up with tears from the chill and the tip of my nose remained numb. It took me 20 minutes to find a parking space at St. Charles Hospital and Rehabilitation Center. I gathered up the three layers of blankets off the back car seat to cover up Elizabeth then I grabbed her baby bag. Elizabeth was wrapped up and snuggled over my shoulder in a crescent shape, her baby bag hung from my right shoulder like a purse. I carefully walked to the exterior door of the chapel, also known as the side entrance, being very cautious not to slip on the black ice. We were there because I had some concerns about Elizabeth. Although she was now two years old she remained the size of a one year old, she was standing (though a bit unsteady) yet did not walk, her attempts to talk were garbled, and she had no interest in potty training. She was unhappy with the slightest change in routine, and while she did smile and gave hugs; her behavior was that of a much younger baby.

What worried me most were her hand tremors, so she was scheduled to be evaluated by a neurologist and other doctors.

As I made my way up the long sidewalk leading towards the chapel door, a woman left the hospital and walked out toward the parking lot, and now she was behind us!

"Elizabeth, Elizabeth!" A soft voice called out. I didn't turn around assuming there was another Elizabeth somewhere in the parking lot. Again I heard "Elizabeth!" you wouldn't even know I had a baby under all the blankets if I wasn't carting a baby bag. This time I turned to find a woman about ten-feet behind me. Our eyes locked as each of us purposefully looked intensely at the other. She was attractive with thick dark brown wavy hair, slightly shorter than me. As I turned toward her, I felt somewhat frightened and surprised as I asked, "Do you know the baby?" The woman replied "I'm Christine, Elizabeth's mother" Oh my God! OOOOH MY GOD!! I couldn't even find the words to describe what I was feeling, I was worried as to what would happen next. I looked around desperately hoping someone was nearby if

I needed help.

After about 45 seconds, the shock wore off and I realized the cold caused condensation to spew from my breath and was clouding in front of my mouth as though I was smoking a cigarette. I invited Christine into the chapel, hoping it would be a safe place for us to talk. I had some pretty bad encounters in the past with birth moms and I wasn't sure what to make of this unplanned and unscheduled meeting. We entered the empty chapel, found a seat in the last pew. Christine started to tell me how appreciative she was for all the wonderful care Armando and I were giving Elizabeth. She talked about her alcoholism and her alcoholic family, stating that her family emigrated from Ireland in the hopes of leaving their alcoholic past behind only to find out it had followed them here to the States. She became teary eyed when she spoke of the day Elizabeth was born and how she tried to stop drinking during her pregnancy.

"The urge to have a beer was overpowering," she told me. She asked me about my family and my children and continued to talk about her lifelong dream of becoming a nurse like me and take care of special needs children.

Christine did most of the talking. She poured her heart out to me all while Elizabeth bounced upon her lap. I really liked this woman, and not just because of the wonderful compliments in her notes. She was humble, open and honest with me-a perfect stranger. Gradually our conversation became more relaxed. Christine was very articulate, comforting, and non-threatening; in fact, she reminded me somewhat of myself. We talked for about

40 minutes before we parted.

I asked Christine how she knew it was Elizabeth under all the blankets. "It was that unique baby bag you had over your shoulder," she explained, "I have never seen anything like it. That's the bag you send with Elizabeth for her home visits. I knew that you were taking her to St. Charles for evaluations from time to time, so I took a chance and called out her name."

Christine went back out into the blistering cold as I continued on to our appointment, that we were now late for. I couldn't believe what had just taken place. This was the first time I had met Christine and she was *NOT* at all what I expected. I often pictured her to look much older than her years, due to her alcohol abuse, with messy hair and wearing dirty clothing covered in cat fur. It was obvious Christine loved Elizabeth. She wore a sincere smile as she caressed Elizabeth in her arms. Her face glowed. I could feel her happiness while Elizabeth sat in her lap and our conversation flowed with ease. I was truly glad I got to meet her. Now I had a face to all the wonderful notes she would send home with Elizabeth.

I never did find out why Christine was there in the first place. I had no way of knowing that this would be the only time we would ever meet.

On February 3, 1992 at 9:00 p.m. Channel 7 aired a movie called The Broken Cord. I had been told by many friends to make sure I watched this made-for-TV movie about Adam, a young Native American boy who was adopted by Michael Dorris, an unmarried college professor. After Adam was adopted, he was diagnosed with fetal alcohol syndrome. Like me, Michael believed that if you surround a child with love, build up their self-esteem and provide therapy to help them thrive, the child will have a better chance of living an independent, productive life. Michael described several heart-breaking scenarios that happened with his son, which were played out in the movie. Michael soon realized that rearing a child with fetal alcohol syndrome is an exhausting continual heightened sense of anticipatory – *"OH MY GOD WHAT NEXT"* moments. He explains he always went to bed tired and woke up the next morning just as tired. Children that are diagnosed with fetal alcohol syndrome suffer from irreversible brain damage. There is no cure! Watching the movie hit home for me and I began to hope that Elizabeth was misdiagnosed, that perhaps she had the lesser diagnosis of fetal alcohol effects instead.

The difference between fetal alcohol effects (FAE) and fetal alcohol syndrome (FAS) is that children with FAE look normal; they don't have the dysmorphic facial features of children with full-blown FAS. Many with FAE have normal IQ's but do have behavior issues at varying degrees. Many suffer from a short attention span, problems with memory, poor judgment, and difficulties with verbal reasoning. They also lack the concept of cause and effect. Since they look "normal," their diagnosis will often go unnoticed by the schools and physicians. It's hard for FAE children to get the special services they need to function adequately. [This information was provided by the Center for Cognitive-Developmental Assessment & Remediation, who offers psychological services for internationally adopted children, as described on

MedicineNet.com.]

On February 19, 1992, Elizabeth went for a checkup with Dr. Ost, her pediatrician. Since she was so tiny for her age (two years, one and a half months), I wasn't surprised to hear that she only weighed 19 pounds and was now 30 inches long. SHE WAS TINY, microcephalic (a small head) and had the classic look of fetal alcohol syndrome, but to me of course she was a perfect beautiful little princess.

On March 10, 1992, I found this note in Elizabeth's diaper bag:

Hi,   *3/10/1992*

Excuse the writing, it's hard to do holding Elizabeth, I can't believe the improvement with her. She has been crawling around here this morning. She is really starting to notice things. She still loves to try to walk. One thing I found out she likes is sherbet. I gave her some this morning and she went wild. I figure maybe it helps her gums.

Once again thanks for giving her such good care. How is the other baby? I hope everything is working out

Thanks again

Chris

On St. Patrick's Day, March 17, 1992, Elizabeth was all dolled up in a new dress that I bought at Sweezy's department store, which was within walking distance from home and my favorite place to buy Elizabeth's clothes and shoes. Everyone knew Elizabeth there. I loved to buy pretty new things for all my girls and I always took Elizabeth with me, often walking and carrying her in an infant body wrap snuggled close to me.

Elizabeth loved her snuggle body wrap; while at first it did nothing to calm her, she now seemed somewhat relaxed although never completely.

At approximately 1:30 p.m. in the afternoon, the transportation driver pulled up, to collect Elizabeth. Her baby bag was packed and ready for a home visit with Mom. A few hours later she was returned to me smelling of cigarette smoke and full of cat hair, and her pretty pink lacy dress was in desperate need of cleaning. I checked the bag for a note and right on top of her toys I found not one but three notes. As I read the notes I couldn't control the river of tears flowing like a tsunami had hit me with full force! I couldn't believe what I was reading, as my knees eventually buckled right out from under me. I rushed to the phone first calling the case worker, then Armando, and then just about everyone and their mother. If no one answered, I went right on to the next person, wanting to tell everyone about the exciting news: Christine has signed the adoption release papers!

I knew Christine had worked really hard on maintaining sobriety and attempting to straighten out her life so she could get her little girl back. This decision had to be absolutely devastating for her, and it wasn't a pleasant thought that my happiness came from Christine's extreme sadness. I wondered what brought her to this point of signing the adoption release.

Signing with a Heavy Hand and Heart

Here are the three notes that Christine put into Elizabeth's bag that day:

Note # 1

Dear Elizabeth   *March 17, 1992*
(St Patty's Day)
I am writing this to you because, after today I will not be able to see you anymore. I am **signing** *the adoption papers today* **with a heavy hand and heart***. I won't be able to see you again until, you are grown. Please believe me this has not been something I've jumped into lightly. I myself don't want to do this. I love you with all my heart and wish so much to have you with me always but, something's can never be. I am unable to give you the home that you need, to provide you with the environment that you need. The people that you are with love you and have been giving you what you have needed since, you were born. They have been your family since you came out of the hospital. They have given you the love and care that you have needed. Please know that this hasn't been the easiest thing for me to do. It has taken me almost 2 ½ yrs to come to signing these adoption papers. I am going to register with the Adoption Information Registry. The New York State Health Department. If when you grow up you wish to find me, my forwarding addresses will be listed with them*
I **love** *you,* **Mommy**

Note # 2

ELIZABETH: FAMILY BACKGROUND,
MEDICAL BACKGROUND.

MOTHERS FAMILY

Mother: (Christine) eye muscles tightened in both eyes at 11 yrs old and 16 yrs old, has 20 / 20 vision, still wears glasses because of muscle weakness in left eye. All childhood diseases, chicken pox, measles etc. I have also had bronchitis. When I was nineteen I was involved in a car accident that injured my back for life. I have had 5 discs removed and had my back fused 4 times, I am also an alcoholic.

Grandmother: alcoholic, death certif. included cancer of the lung (Brigit JRK)

Grandfather: alcoholic, death certif. included cancer of the blood (Walter Joseph K Jr.)

Great-grandmother: (Catherine K) diabetic, heart disease, over weight.

Great-grandfather: Walter Joseph K. Sr.: alcoholic, heart disease

I have no brothers and sisters so, Elizabeth you have no aunts and uncles.

Your great-grandparents on my mother's side were: William and Helena R. I never knew them, my grandfather died of lung cancer and my grandmother was killed in a fire when I was two. I do know that they came from Ireland to start a new life. Your great-

> *grandfather was born in Scotland but, raised in Ireland. Your great grandmother was born in Ireland. They came to America in the 1920's. They had four children and opened a pet shop. So if you love animals it's in your blood.*
>
> *I really know nothing about your father's side of the family. His name is Robert F.H. Jr. His father has diabetes*

Note # 3

> *½ sister Sue, lives with natural father Michael B. and step mother... She will graduate 6/92 high school. Has full scholarship to Syracuse Univ. Wants to be a veterinarian.*
>
> *Ma grand-father K. died of C.H.F. also had cancer*
> *Ma grand-mother Nee .R. died of lung cancer 1991*
> *Christine married Michael B 1971-1979*
> *Married Harry W. 1990*
> *Christine is an only child 6-21-52*

This would be the last time I heard from Christine. She had requested an open adoption and planned to be in court on adoption day.

The official letter came to us shortly after the review date on 7/10/1992 and read: Summary of review (including recommendations): The permanency planning goal for Elizabeth has been changed from Discharge to Parent to Adoption because Elizabeth was legally freed for adoption on 3/17/1992 by court order. Elizabeth was born with fetal alcohol syndrome, she is cognitively and developmentally delayed. She continues to thrive in the foster home of Mr. and Mrs. Torres where she receives excellent care and nurturing. Elizabeth was placed in this home directly after she was born and discharged from the hospital. Mr. and Mrs. Torres have signed the Intent to adopt form, and the adoption home study has been completed and the legalization process has begun.

My case worker guided us to the steps toward adoption for both Elizabeth and Tiffany. I was worried about Tiffany's birth mother putting a stop to the adoption. I was told by one of the case workers that Tiffany's birth mother didn't want me to adopt her because I am Caucasian. She wanted Tiffany to be adopted into an African American family—in order to "learn about her African American culture." The problem was, there just weren't enough black families at that time that were able to adopt a child with a disability.

Love is color blind! Elizabeth and Tiffany had become very close buddies by then. Tiffany seemed to be the only one that understood Elizabeth's very garbled speech. I wish I had recorded some of their conversations. Elizabeth garbled back and forth while Tiffany listened intently for long periods of time. Sometimes I was sure they were talking in code.

On August 24, 1992, I met with the adoption lawyer Kevin Powers, and on September 22, 1992 we had a visit from Mrs. Garrally, the adoption case worker who had taken over our case.

She was there to prepare us for adoption. This was the day I asked permission to start calling the girls by their new names, my request was granted. Elizabeth was now Chanel (a name given to her by my sister, Jorain) and Tiffany was now Alonna (a name fit for a princess!)

Soon after, I received written permission in the mail, so Chanel and Alonna began using their new names at school, doctor's appointments and therapy, as well as at home. To help them adapt, we called them by their pre-adoptive names three to four times, followed by using their chosen names, then went back to three to four times with their pre-adoptive names; gradually lessening the use of Tiffany and Elizabeth. The transition went much easier than I thought it would.

Thanksgiving was especially wonderful that year, as our family was about to officially get bigger. We prepared all of our favorite foods, and celebrated big. Although Chanel was just shy of two years old, she really enjoyed our family tradition of taking turns around the table letting everyone know what he or she was most grateful for. This year we were all grateful for the two beautiful little girls that sat in front of us. Alonna and Chanel!

Christmas was as big as ever, in the "Torres Way." This year along with many other requested gifts, Armando and I bought the girls a fish bowl and one fish each. Chanel's fish was deep blue and she named it Flounder, and Alonna's fish was purple (her favorite color) and she named it Magenta. While visiting one of my neighbors, I received a phone call from one of my older daughters informing me that Chanel's fish was missing and nowhere to be found. I rushed home to find that the fish had somehow made its way out of the fish bowl and onto the floor. I quickly picked up the limp fish and put it back into the water. I didn't tell Chanel that her fish was dead, but she knew something was up. She inquisitively asked in her garbled voice, "Why does he look so funny?"

I replied, "He's sleeping." I quickly bought a new fish, but I couldn't find a blue one so this one was red. I told Chanel that our fish were very special and they changed color when they wanted to change their outfit.

CHAPTER EIGHT:

WHAT IS FETAL ALCOHOL SYNDROME

When coping with the behavioral issues in a child with fetal alcohol syndrome, or reading about them as you are, it is easy to forget that these are manifestations of the physiological brain damage caused by alcohol use during pregnancy, rather than willful misconduct on the part of the child. For that reason, I am pausing Chanel's story to insert a brief description of fetal alcohol syndrome (FAS) so that you will have a better understanding of Chanel and the life-long sentence she must endure.

I have become passionate about teaching others about fetal alcohol syndrome, yet it seems there is never enough time to say it all. Writing this book has helped me meet this challenge, and has also been extremely cathartic. As you'll hear about later, Chanel has participated in this passion project in a way I could have never imagined.

Fetal alcohol syndrome is a birth defect that is 100 percent preventable just by abstaining from drinking any alcoholic beverages while pregnant.

Alcohol has a teratogenic effect on the embryo and the fetus, causing permanent damage. There is NO cure and the effects last a lifetime. Many victims of fetal alcohol syndrome are undiagnosed.

According to Gail Harris, one of the founders of the FAS Community Resource Center in Tucson, Arizona states that nothing, not even crack cocaine, is as devastating to a fetus as alcohol. Alcohol does more damage to a developing brain and body than any other illegal drug (Alcohol's toll on the unborn is the worst of any drug." Southern Arizona Online). It's not a genetic disorder so it cannot be passed down from generation to generation. It is found in all racial and socio-economic groups.

When a pregnant woman consumes alcohol such as beer, wine or any mixed drink, the alcohol crosses the placenta freely, directly reaching the embryo or fetus. There is no amount of alcohol use during pregnancy that has been proven to be completely safe. Even small amounts of alcohol can be harmful. The severity of the defect varies from victim to victim, depending on several factors; the amount consumed, the timing of the consumption (whether in the first, second or third trimester of pregnancy), whether the pregnant woman has eaten any food while drinking and numerous other factors. Some doctors think an occasional drink while pregnant produces no risk to the fetus, while Linda Nicholson, a genetic counselor states: "We don't know how much alcohol is safe so we just say, don't drink at all."

Alcohol causes more neurological damage to the developing baby than any other substance. The CDC estimates that 0.5 to 2.0 cases per 1,000 live births are born with fetal alcohol syndrome in the United States every year. It is a known fact that alcohol can have a profound effect even very early in pregnancy. Since women don't often know they are pregnant early on, it's best to stop drinking while you are planning to become pregnant. Symptoms of fetal alcohol syndrome:

1. Distinctive facial features such as, small eyes, thin upper lip missing or indistinct philtrum (the area above the upper lip leading up to the nose), flat-mid face, and larger than usual malformed ears.

2. Microcephaly (a small head).

3. Slow physical growth before and after birth.

4. Learning disorders.

5. Poor coordination.

6. Abnormal behavior: such as a short attention span, distractibility, hyperactivity, poor impulse control, anxiety, inability to grasp the concept of cause and effect, and repeating the same bad behavior over and over again.

7. Difficulty with math skills.

8. Poor ability to think abstractly as opposed to concretely.

9. Speech problems.

10. Stubbornness.

11. Fearlessness.

12. Overstimulation.

13. Depression.

14. Behaviors such as stealing and lying/fibbing.

15. Inability to handle money appropriately for their age, and even as adults tending to spend any money they earn, without regard to saving for tomorrow or setting aside money they'll need for necessities.

Victims of fetal alcohol syndrome have many other behavioral characteristics; socially they are seen as outgoing and engaging, yet they are often perceived by others as intrusive, overly talkative, and unaware of social cues. They have poor social judgment. Many of them are hungry for attention, good or bad. They have difficulty maintaining friendships due to their social immaturity.

As a parent of a child with fetal alcohol syndrome, I found the following suggestions from the Mayo Clinic website very helpful when dealing with the behavioral problems associated with FAS.

1. Maintain a daily routine.

2. Give simple one-step rules and limits, being consistent when enforcing the rules.

3. Reward acceptable behavior.

4. Guard against others taking advantage of them. Victims of fetal alcohol syndrome are vulnerable, and in social groups, they are often followers.

5. Be careful when choosing who will supervise, baby sit or befriend your child.

6. Provide a stable, nurturing home. Children with fetal alcohol syndrome are more sensitive than other children to disruptions, changes or routines. Be a good role-model.

7. Take note of your child's strengths and talents.

8. Accept your child's limitations.

9. Be consistent with everything (discipline, school, behaviors etc.):

   a.   Avoid threats

   b.   Redirect behavior

   c.   Intervene before behavior escalates

Please note that fetal alcohol syndrome is a complex diagnosis, and this is only a very brief explanation. Now that you know a bit more about fetal alcohol syndrome, you will be able to better understand Chanel and her everyday struggles.

CHAPTER NINE:

STICKY FINGERS

It was January 1993 and Chanel had become a very curious little girl. She was finally walking and as long as the terrain was smooth she was becoming steadier on her feet. Her chronological age was three but her developmental age was slightly under two.

One day, I started to notice that strange things were happening. I was missing things. I knew exactly where I'd put something, but then when I went to get it, it was gone. Yet Chanel always seemed to know where my missing things were. One Tuesday I was missing my schedule book. I was very upset, franticly searching the house, starting with all the usual places and then moving on to every little nook and cranny in the house. Suddenly Chanel told me "I know where it is Mommy. Come I show you," in her continuous garbled voice. She took me to one of the second floor bathrooms and dragged a step-ladder in front of an 8-foot-tall linen closet. She climbed like a monkey until she reached the very top, crawled into the cubby hole of the top shelf, stretched and stretched until she could reach the very back, then she pulled out my schedule book. I completely forgot how important my diary entries were. My mouth fell open in disbelief before I could finally bring myself to ask Chanel; "How did my book get all the way up there?" Chanel replied, "I don't know Mommy, it just got there." I didn't believe a three year-old could have the concept of ownership, so I didn't consider this to be stealing. I wasn't exactly sure how to handle this, and I certainly didn't want to overreact so I tried to remain calm, and I just praised her for helping me find my book.

Later on in the day while Chanel was playing in the back-yard, I climbed up the ladder and reached into that top shelf, hoping to find other treasures that I had been missing. There were none, but incidents like this continued to happen through the years.

In May 1993, Armando and I were informed that Alonna's

Alonna and Chanel

birth mother had passed. No further details were given to us. We received a list of Alonna's four biological brothers' and one sister with their full names and birth dates, as well as a photo of each child. The most precious photo was one of Alonna sitting on her birth mother's lap. We decided not to tell Alonna the sad news at this time. Alonna didn't remember her mother, grandmother, brothers or her sister or any of the home visits. Her last home visit was when she was seventeen months old. Alonna's birth mother had given her a black baby doll, which Alonna held closely each night before going to sleep, and she still has that doll today.

One day after a long weekend, Chanel was waiting for the school bus to take her to school. Chanel (still with her somewhat garbled speech) asked for a dollar, saying, "I want a school snack." As I reached into my pocket to pull out the money, a few $1 bills, a $5 bill and a $100 bill flurried onto the floor like snowflakes. Chanel quickly scooped up the money and handed the bills to me. She asked for the $100 bill, looking inquisitively at the picture on it and pointing to the man, I pulled a $1 bill out of the pile and handed it to her. She smiled as I put the rest of the bills safely in my pocket. The bus arrived, Chanel got her usual hugs and kisses, as I stood there at the curb and waved goodbye to her. Finally, mommy time!

As I was eating my breakfast at the kitchen table, attempting to unwind in this suddenly peaceful environment, my phone rang. It was the bus driver, who asked, "Did you know that Chanel has a $100 bill and she's showing it off to all her friends?"

I quickly rummaged through my pockets, and sure enough the $100 bill was missing. I was perplexed and baffled. How did she do that? Houdini! The bus driver said that he wasn't far and he would bring the money back. Once again I didn't have a clue how to handle this situation.

Should I punish her, and if so, how?

I had never even scolded her, let alone punish her. She was not capable of knowing the monetary difference between a $1 bill and a $100 bill. What she had noticed was that she liked "that man" better, pointing to the picture of Benjamin Franklin. So I explained to Chanel that this was wrong, and this behavior would not be tolerated in the future. I gave her a hug and sent her on her way, and that was it.

At the age of 4 ½ years old, Chanel was still in diapers, she showed no interest in potty train-ing like all her peers. She was now walking but still unable to navigate stairs. The tremors in her hands were more pronounced and I no-ticed some garbled stuttering. I was assured by the neurologist and pediatricians that this was due to her diagnosis of fetal alcohol

Armando and Chanel

syndrome, "Nothing to worry about, most likely from her ner-vousness." A battery of neurological testing showed no need for any new intervention at this time. We were advised to continue with the occupational services at the St. Charles Early Interven-tion Program, with an increase of occupational therapy sessions from two times a week to three.

Not long after the $100 bill incident, I took Chanel shopping at one of my favorite stores in town. As we walked through the store with a shopping cart, Chanel took a few items off the shelves and put them in my cart. I immediately told her, "We don't need this," and I put each item back from where she had taken them. I paid for our items at the register and we left the store. Much to my surprise, when we got home Chanel handed me a belt. When I asked her where she got the belt she replied, "From the store."

"Do you realize this is stealing? Stealing is when you take something without permission, something that doesn't belong to you."

"I'm so sorry, Mommy, I didn't mean to do it, I thought you wanted it."

In a firm voice I told Chanel: "We have to go back to the store and return this, okay?"

"No, Mommy, please, no, no, I can't. I don't want to get in trouble. Please, I can't bring it back," Chanel pleaded.

"The store has cameras all over, they saw you take the belt. The manager will be calling us soon with instructions for us to return it. It's best we take the belt back to the store before they call."

I put Chanel in the car and drove her back to the department store. When I attempted to get her out of the car she resisted and cried loudly and intensely, until her face turned dusky blue. People driving nearby slowed down to see what was going on. Some gave me dirty looks as though I was doing something wrong. I had to nip this in the bud quickly, before it became an even bigger problem. I continued to be firm and did not buckle as Chanel's bawling continued.

I had to just about drag her into the store to return the merchandise. I asked for the manager, and then asked Chanel to apologize for taking something that didn't belong to her.

She was very upset.

You can't imagine how badly I wanted to just hug her and say we could forget the whole thing. Don't worry, I didn't.

.

CHAPTER TEN:

THE WEDDING

Chanel ready for
wedding trouble

It was May 16, 1993; all my favorite colors were in full bloom. Rhododendrons and azalea bushes were all over Patchogue, but especially noticeable on Jayne Ave. I made sure to plant bulbs in various colors in the prior year, hoping the timing would be right and praying they would come into full bloom for this remarkable day.

Bright red, pink, yellow and white flowers aligned the driveway. The timing WAS perfect! Our yard was full of assorted colors. Our family came from near and far, all to celebrate a magnificent union. Trudy (my first born) and Carlos were getting married, after dating for eight years.

Alonna and Chanel were the flower girls. Many of my family members would be meeting them for the first time, though my letters and phone conversations for the past couple of years had been obsessed with the girls' beauty and how much I loved them. One by one our guests arrived and introduced themselves to the children, complimenting me on how charming and polite the girls were, before retreating to their hotel with the anticipation of the following day's big wedding.

Both girls awoke at 6:00 a.m. all excited about wearing their extravagant Victorian ankle length deep plum colored gowns to match the bridesmaids dresses. They would each be carrying an adorable bouquet of flowers, with ribbon streamers that flowed down from the front of the perfectly arranged posies.

It was on this day when I first realized that Chanel's diagnosis of fetal alcohol syndrome was for real. Her behavioral symptoms were more evident than ever. I needed to remind myself throughout this important day, "She has fetal alcohol syndrome and to no fault of her own." I remained calm and did my best not to allow Chanel's behaviors to overshadow this glorious ceremony that had taken us well over a year to plan. I'm not sure if her behaviors were stemming from over-stimulation or maybe she was just tired, but whatever the reason, the fetal alcohol syndrome was up front and center. Even before she got dressed, Chanel was already whiny and demanding my attention, which lead into a total meltdown (and I was about to join her). All Armando and I wanted to do was to show off what a wonderful job we were doing rais-

Susan W and the Torres daughters

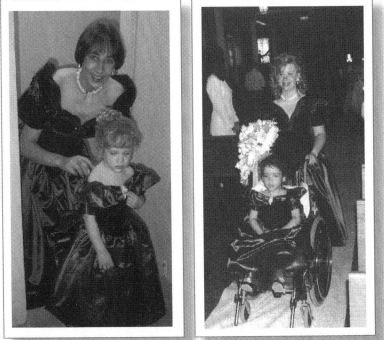

Dana and Chanel   Susan W and Alonna

Aunt Brenda helping Trudy with her wedding gown (above)

ing our special needs children. I had always thought if you surrounded a child with enough love, and provided them with a happy healthy environment they could overcome anything.

On this day, Chanel's poor impulse control had gone awry, she was fidgety and fearless, and had not been able to focus on what was going on around her. I didn't know how she was going to manage walking down the aisle carrying the bouquet of flow-

Sondra and Alonna

ers. In just a few hours her personal sitter, Kristy, would arrive to take over tending to her every need. Our family had known Kristy for several years now. She was a classmate and friend of one of our daughters. She was great with Chanel, but at this point I wasn't sure if even she was going to be able to handle her. I just had to trust my instincts.

Kristy arrived just as my sister Brenda was summoning me to the second floor bedroom where she wanted me to help my beautiful daughter Trudy put on her wedding gown.

One by one my family filed into the limousines, my mother (Rosina Morgan) and my daughters all sliding into the back seat for the short drive to the church.

As we all gathered in front of the quaint little chapel of St. Francis De Sales Church in Patchogue, (where Trudy taught CCD lessons for several years) Chanel kept darting off into the large crowd of friends, family, co-workers, neighbors and bystanders. My nerves were on fire with fear that she would run onto the very busy South Ocean Avenue. Just as soon as I caught up to her, she would run off again. She appeared completely disconnected from what was going on around her! Luckily, her sitter quickly came to the rescue and took Chanel by the hand into the church, sitting with her in one of the back pews to calm her down. With the stress of managing Chanel off my shoulders, I welled up with tears at the magnitude of the day. I turned toward the back of the church and peeked through the large double doors of the chapel and saw the most beautiful woman in the world get out of a white polished Rolls Royce, dressed in an absolutely gorgeous beaded

Victorian wedding gown fit for a princess; her father at her side. The organ music was playing the wedding song.

Trudy and Armando entered the chapel, while Alonna wheeled her chair down the aisle just ahead of them. She led the procession alone, without Chanel by her side as originally planned. Behind Alonna was Susan W. (Trudy's childhood friend and maid-of-honor). The organ music was stimulating millions of goose-bumps from my head to my toes. After a brief moment of anticipatory silence, my cousin Linda's angelic voice filled the cozy chapel and beyond. My heart was racing as I choked back tears. I heard a very brief loud cry that was quickly controlled. I looked around to see who it was, and of course it was my second born, Alexa. Her emotions were contagious, as sniffles were heard throughout the chapel, but none were as loud as Alexa's.

Suddenly I heard a commotion from the direction of the back pew. It was Chanel, climbing under the bench and over the bench, running away from the sitter. The chapel was quiet other than Chanel's playful yet garbled voice yelling out, "Catch me!" Everyone continued to focus on Trudy and Carlos at the front of the church. Kristy and Chanel quickly retreated through the large double doors of the chapel, but we could still hear Chanel incessantly running around the front yard and the sidewalk calling out to Kristy, "Catch me, if you can!" I focused on enjoying the rest of this special day although I couldn't completely set aside my concerns that Chanel could get hurt out there.

After Trudy and Carlos said their vows, the chapel emptied out into the front yard as everyone lined up to wish the bride and groom well. Chanel had other plans. She proceeded to have a full-blown tantrum. I did my best to remember what a friend once told me: a tantrum is like a Broadway show, if no one shows up to watch it, the show doesn't take place. After the wedding photos were taken, I instructed the sitter to take Chanel home. I didn't think it was safe for Chanel to join us at the reception.

We partied until late at night stopping several times to call home and check on Chanel.

From that day on, those behavior issues persisted and new ones arrived monthly. Whenever I mentioned these behaviors to the pediatrician he didn't seem to know what to make of them. "She has fetal alcohol syndrome," he told me, advising me to see the behavior specialist she was assigned to at school.

CHAPTER ELEVEN:

CPS THREAT AND NIGHTTIME ADVENTURES

Buying toys was something I loved to do whenever I got the chance, which was obvious by looking at all the toys strewn all over our home and out in the yard. Toys piled on top of more toys. One day, Alonna and Chanel were playing with blocks and pull toys. I heard one of the girls playing with a toy drum. Next I heard Alonna yelling out "M~O~M," (in a musical tone of voice) "Chanel broke my leg." I glanced into the room and told the girls to play nice as I walked off; Alonna gave me one of her special sweet smiles. When I checked on the girls approximately twenty minutes later, as I did several times through the afternoon, I scooped Alonna up for a fresh diaper change. As I laid her on the sofa and removed her long pants it was obvious something was wrong—REALLY WRONG! ALONNA'S LEG WAS WARM, RED AND EDEMATOUS-all classic signs for a fracture.

"OH my God!! OOH MY GOD!" I yelled out to Alonna, "I think your leg is broken"

Alonna put her hand on her hip and sweetly said "I told you Mommy, Chanel broke my leg. She dropped the drum on my leg."

I was so frightened I didn't know who to call first. Thankfully, Alonna's physical therapist was due to come for her physical therapy session in five minutes. As I waited for

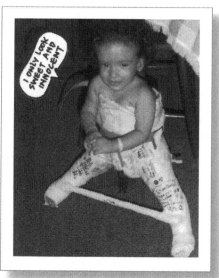

Alonna in one of her many spica casts

the therapist I frantically called Dr Crestman (Alonna's orthopedist), his attempts to calm me down were fruitless! He continued to tell me, "calm down, get Alonna to St Charles ER "I will call them ahead of time, they will be waiting for you."

Just as I hung up the phone Alonna's physical therapist arrived. She knew immediately something wasn't right. Just two months or so prior to this day Dr. Crestman had done bilateral hip replacements for Alonna, after which she was placed in a spica (full body) cast. In fact, it had only been two weeks since the cast was removed. I scooped Alonna up very carefully; making sure her leg braces were locked to stabilize her legs, and then I laid her on the back seat of my car and fastened the seat belts. Then we were off to St Charles ER for the twenty-minute nerve wracking drive. I was so distraught I felt sick to my stomach. I parked my car in the special ER parking area. As Port Jefferson is somewhat hilly, carrying Alonna from the car to the ER was torturous. As I entered the hospital and walked up to the triage area of the ER I explained to the nurse, "Dr. Crestman called ahead, they are waiting for us in the back." When the nurse turned around and asked if anyone had heard from Dr. Crestman, they all replied "No." I continued to insist that he had called, despite not one nurse being able to report that they did receive a call from him. The triage nurse made several attempts to reach someone from orthopedics, but was unsuccessful. I was guided to the back patient care area, where several nurses and two doctors came to Alonna's aid and rushed her off for an x-ray. An Asian doctor approached me and asked in a firm voice "WHAT HAPPENED?" With my body and voice quivering, I explained that Chanel had dropped the toy drum onto Alonna's leg. My legs were about to give out on me. I was so upset, I could hardly stand up. The Doctor was questioning me intensely and the more he did, it was obvious he believed something tragic had happened. Alonna was whisked off to an orthopedic room upstairs and placed in traction. A security guard asked me to leave the hospital and go directly home. I cried uncontrollably as I drove back to Patchogue. Two hours later as I was on the phone with one of my sisters, I heard a very loud BANG, BANG, BANG on the upper most part of the front door. Through the window pane I saw a badge being held flat against the glass. I was so frightened I wanted to wet my pants!

"Child protection services" the voice called out firmly.

All I could think was, "I have been a foster parent for a long time. It is my job to protect children from harm. How can this be happening? I opened the door and escorted the officer into the living room, describing to him exactly what had happened. On request, I gave him the phone number of Barbara, our case worker. The very next morning, Barbara called me. "I have some sad news that is going to make you feel good" she said. Hmmm, that didn't make a bit of sense. Barbara recounted a story of another little foster boy who also had hip surgery and was placed in a spica cast. Two weeks later his leg was also fractured. She went on to explain that there was a medical reason that children with spina bifida are susceptible to fractures. It wasn't my fault, nor was it Chanel's fault! The above story was told to Barbara by the orthopedist. I felt so sorry for the other little boy, but I must admit, I was extremely relieved. The next thing I knew, the case was dropped with no further interaction from CPS other than a letter a few weeks later explaining that the case was unfounded. Alonna fractured her legs several more times in the next few years (without Chanel's help, I might add) though none were as bad as the above experience.

On August 28, 1993, Trudy and Carlos moved from their apartment in NY to Florida to start a new life. Of course I wasn't happy about the move, especially knowing there was NO way we would ever move to Florida. I had built up a good rapport with the pediatric doctors here in New York. The children received the best services from early intervention, we lived in the best neighborhood, and Armando and I both had great jobs so there was no reason to move. Still I walked around sullenly for a long time and couldn't get myself out of the somber mood that held me captive. I desperately wanted to be there when Trudy and Carlos had their first baby. I had no way of knowing when that would happen.

On October 29 1993, I resigned from my agency nursing job and took on steady employment at Brookhaven Health Care Facility working the 11 p.m.-7 a.m. shift. This employment offered a full health benefit package as well as a well-crafted retirement plan. At this point, Chanel was finally sleeping through most of the night. Alonna's fractured leg healed and her cast was about to be removed. Alonna and Chanel continued to attend school during the day, while I slept.

Sometime in the month of October, on one of my nights off from work, I was startled as I entered the kitchen at 2:00 a.m. to get a drink, I found Chanel sitting on top of the refrigerator with a VERY large knife in her mouth as she licked icing off the sharp blade. Earlier that day we had bought a frozen ice-cream cake. Armando used the large knife to cut the cake and then placed it far behind the kitchen sink. To date we still haven't figured out how Chanel was able to get the knife. To protect Chanel, the very next morning I purchased several motion detectors from Radio Shack, and placed them strategically throughout our home. Whenever she left her room we were alerted by the loud alarm. The other alarms were backups just in case the one over her door failed. Much to our surprise, the alarm over her door went off several times a night. We were completely unaware of how much she was wandering around the house at night while we slept.

When we questioned Chanel about where she was going, she always answered, "I don't know, I'm just not tired." After three months of having Armando peek in on her every time she left her room and set off the alarm, she finally gave up leaving her room in the middle of the night. Peace at last!

CHAPTER TWELVE:

ADOPTION DAY

Friday, November 12, 1993, the girls woke up early. Chanel ran into Alonna's room yelling, "Get up! GET UP, HURRY!" They were both excited because this was a very special day. Big sister Jessica dressed them in their Sunday best and fixed their hair with ribbons and bows. They received first class-five star pampering treatment. We were all so excited and wanted to share our exciting news with the world. We posted a huge sign in our front yard that said "ADOPTED" and tied colorful balloons around several of our trees. Chanel giggled each time a car passed and blew the horn to acknowledge our celebration. As we all piled into the van and headed off to the Central Islip Family Court Complex and into the Cohalan building, I listened to the girls giggling from the back seat. Jessica and Dana had driven separately. The parking lot was usually packed, but on this day we had our choice of spots. The girls were excited and nervous and asked the cutest questions. Security was tight; we had to put our purses through the metal detector before entering the X-ray tunnel. They were especially curious about why we had to walk through a "tunnel" and take everything out of our pockets before we could enter the court building.

I looked around every corner and back to the next searching for Christine, but she was nowhere to be found. She had requested an open adoption and had promised to be here. It couldn't be an open adoption if she didn't show up.

I heard our names being paged: "TORRES FAMILY!" Just as soon as little Chanel heard our names being called, she bolted! My family and I frantically chased after her as she crawled on the floor, under the chairs and on to the next row of seats. She was laughing, clearly enjoying the fact that she was making five adults look like total fools as we chased after her. Many other adoptive families were now in the waiting area with us, watching this circus take place. Finally I nabbed her, and soon we were sitting back down with our lawyer. He spread out some papers on a bench so he could go over some things with us. Chanel accidentally kicked all the papers onto the floor that were once laid out in nice neat and organized piles, narrowly missing a cup of coffee. I apologized as I attempted to redirect Chanel's energy."

"Come on, Chanel, let's go, they called our name, we're up next! This is your special day. You're going to be all ours shortly." Our name was paged again. Our family was ushered into closed chambers. The judge sat at the far end of the table, he welcomed each one of us; Athena the adoption case worker, our lawyer, daughters Dana and Jessica and of course Armando and myself but most importantly Chanel and Alonna. Armando and I sat right next to the judge for ease of signing the many papers that would lead us into a LIFELONG COMMITMENT that we both took very seriously. Armando and I were both so grateful for this opportunity to share our lives with these two very special little girls.

I suppose this was not the right time to reflect back on something one of Chanel's early Intervention teachers once told me but it happened so spontaneously:

"Most victims of fetal alcohol syndrome will never drive a car, complete high school or attend college. Most will never move out of the family home or be able to live without close supervision for the rest of their lives. Adoption is not a temporary transferring of parental responsibilities," she continued, "I have seen the toll fetal alcohol syndrome victims take on their families. They will change your life in a way you cannot imagine. The road ahead is unpredictable."

Although I had also heard similar stories from others: I chose to take all the negative talk about fetal alcohol syndrome and turn it into positive motivation. Realistically, I knew the road we would travel as a family in the next few years was not going to be an easy one, but once we signed those papers, it would be our job to provide a positive atmosphere for generating good behavior. Boy, did I still have a lot to learn about fetal alcohol syndrome! Hearing about it and experiencing its wrath was daunting.

As I snapped back to the present moment, I reminded myself

that we were ready to take on whatever challenges awaited us. I knew we were prepared to stick by Chanel for the good, the bad and the unpredictable. Although Chanel was hyperactive and had some other behavior issues, she was very sincere with her apologies. Armando and I signed the adoption papers with our heads held high and our hearts filled with promise.

When we returned home we celebrated with cake and milk, as the girls opened up some gifts from the family. I could now let out a sigh of relief! "They're mine, ALL MINE! No one can take them from me. We are now a family of nine!" Armando, Sondra, Trudy, Alexa, Jessica, Dana and Brendalyn could welcome Alonna and Chanel as permanent members of the Torres family.

I never heard from Christine again, and neither did the case worker. We lost all contact with her.

Chanel's behaviors had started occurring more frequently by the middle of 1994, so we had her evaluated at Stony Brook hospital. The diagnosis of fetal alcohol syndrome would be confirmed! This came as no surprise to me, but nonetheless, it was still painful to hear. We brought Chanel to this clinic for almost weekly visits for behavior modification. On one of our visits, a doctor entered the room and asked for my permission to allow the student doctors to examine Chanel. I agreed, with the silent hope that if they learned something from this exam, we would all gain from it. Chanel was on the examining table; one by one the students came in. Surrounding the table, they pointed at her face, exclaiming to each other, "look at her small head, her tiny body, her weight and height is way below where it should be." Chanel was smiling and fidgeting almost nonstop, grabbing at their stethoscopes and neckties and reaching for hugs from these complete strangers. Her restlessness kept me on a heightened sense of alert, for fear she would fall off the examining table.

The merry-go-round of doctors lasted for a good fifteen minutes before they all paraded out of the room, leaving me bewildered with my thoughts that ran wild, "GEE WHIZ, she was their guinea pig. Did I do the right thing by allowing them to look at her like some sort of specimen?"

The instructor remained in the room to thank me for allowing the students to examine Chanel. "She is lovely," he declared.

On the ride home, I played soft children's music to lighten up the mood and to hopefully calm Chanel down.

CHAPTER THIRTEEN:

IMAGINARY FRIENDS
EARLY 1995

We were introduced to Chanel's three new friends: Gea-Gea, Margaret, and Petey, her imaginary companions. She talked to them when she was seeking comfort or when she was feeling lonely, sad or lost and needed a friend. She bossed them around and blamed them when something went wrong."They did it Mommy, they did it," she proclaimed, "All of them, they took the book off the table Mommy, I didn't do it." Sometimes when we walked into town, she called out to them one at a time, "C'mon, GeaGea and Margaret, catch up to Petey and me," as she turned to look behind her. Sometimes she asked me to stop and "give them a chance to catch up!" At night in her room, she made up stories for them about beautiful places and pretty trees they could climb.

I wasn't sure what to make of this, but the pediatrician assured me this behavior was normal, "Lots of children have imaginary friends. This will stop by the time she is five or six years old." I accepted that this was all part of Chanel's creative and healthy imagination and overall development. Chanel didn't have any close friends at school, in our neighborhood or at our library reading club. She commonly stayed to herself off to the side when she was around other children. Her poor social skills and learning disabilities often got in the way of establishing and maintaining friendships. On a few occasions I would invite children from her class over for a play date but they never showed up. GeaGea, Margaret and Petey were her only close friends.

Chanel's favorite place to be alone with her three friends was right outside our house, between Gail's home and ours. Our flowering crab apple tree had low-lying branches that were perfect for climbing. She would climb into that tree like a monkey and sit there for long periods of time, swinging from branch to branch calling out to her friends to chase her.

CHAPTER FOURTEEN:

AN FAS EDUCATION FOR RICKY'S UNCLE

On a Monday morning, I called the eyeglass store for the fourth time, to ask whether Chanel's eyeglasses were in. A gentleman answered the phone and said the glasses were there. When he asked to confirm the name and date of birth, I told him, "Chanel Torres, December 31, 1989." "Wait a minute," he sighed, I think they ordered the wrong size, the pair of glasses we have here in the store are for a six–twelve month old"

"NO, no that's the right size," I assured him. "Chanel is so petite we can't even get a good fitting bike helmet for her. "The salesman wasn't convinced and asked us to come in for another fitting.

Chanel called out to Petey, Margaret and GeaGea to get in the back seat of the car and she made sure they each put their seat belts on, checking Petey, then Margaret and finally GeaGea. It was a 15-minute drive to the eyeglass store. The salesman chuckled as he saw that the eyeglasses did indeed fit Chanel. "She has fetal alcohol syndrome" I explained. Children with fetal alcohol syndrome are microcephalic; it's a medical condition in which the circumference of the head is smaller than normal because the brain hasn't developed properly in utero, or has stopped growing, due to the birth mom's consumption of alcohol while she was pregnant."

With a surprised look he revealed that he had a nephew with fetal alcohol syndrome. He pulled out his wallet and showed me several pictures of his nephew. "They look like relatives" he sighed;" "I guess it's the fetal alcohol syndrome. My nephew, Ricky, sure is a challenge; sometimes his behaviors are out of control. He just started on medication for ADHD. He's eight years old and can't ride a bike yet. My sister-in-law was an alcoholic and drank while she was pregnant but stopped when she was about five months along, and now little Ricky has to pay the price."

"Listen," I interjected, determined to put the conversation on a positive note, "Statistically, children with FAS have a somewhat predictable course or path that they will follow. But my plan, my dream, and my hope is that Chanel will be among the many that beats the odds. Realistically, I know it won't be an easy path that Chanel will endure. But I'm not going to let medical guidelines on fetal alcohol syndrome be her fate! I'm determined to be optimistic, enthusiastic and passionate about these pathways, however convoluted they may be. The more negativity I read about fetal alcohol syndrome, the more fired up I get to inspire Chanel and focus on the things she is best at. Your nephew and Chanel will face many more obstacles and road blocks than other children. Obstacles can drain their energy and keep them from becoming productive members of society if we allow that to happen. Or, these obstacles could very well be the stepping stones to their future. At this point the future is unknown for Chanel, as it is for your nephew, but I am learning right alongside her. Together Chanel and I can beat this! "

"Fetal alcohol syndrome is irreversible. Therapy and love will not undo the brain damage that took place in the uterus, but it can lessen the amount of untoward behaviors." The salesman thanked me for all the information and stated that he would share this advice with his brother.

CHAPTER FIFTEEN:

LAST YEAR AT ST. CHARLES EARLY INTERVENTION PROGRAM

Chanel's last year in St. Charles Early Intervention Program was nearing the end. This program had provided a variety of therapy and gave supportive services for Chanel and our family, giving her the building blocks needed for a smooth transition into kindergarten and the following years. The moving up ceremony began at 10:00 a.m.; Chanel was excited about her family attending the ceremony. She looked beautiful as always, with her thick curly blondish hair down to her waist. She was to perform a song, with her teacher sitting right next to her for close supervision; she had been practicing for weeks. "YOU ARE SPEEEEECIAL, SPEEEEECIAL, SPECIAL IN EVERY WAY." During her performance, every now and then I caught her looking in my direction, making sure I was watching her. When the ceremony was over

97

she scrambled over to me, calling, "Did you see me Mommy? Did you? Did you?" Chanel was a pleaser, and she especially loved to please me.

After the ceremony was over I took the girls on a shopping spree in Patchogue. I always loved to dress the girls in pretty dresses from Sweezy's Department store; pink, lavender, soft yellow, powder blue, lacy with lots of bows and small petite beading. Polly Flinders puckered dresses were my favorite. I couldn't get enough of my little girls. They were being lavished with love and attention and all the beautiful things little girls could want.

After shopping the girls helped me put all the pretty new dresses away then off they went to play with their new toys.

I loved to go into my girls' closets and stare at the collection of beautiful clothes along with the large array of shoes in different colors and styles. On the first shelf of the closet was a large box filled with adorable hair bows

Chanel's new room

and barrettes in various colors to match the colored dresses and socks. At the foot of Chanel's bed was a neatly positioned pink toy box, filled with many different girly toys, and a table with two cute little chairs and a tea set for two. On Chanel's second floor bedroom wall I had painted a ceiling-to-floor mural of a country home, with a black kitten peaking out of the second floor window while a light brown cat was on the look-out from the first floor window. Beautiful flowers abounded through the front yard. To the right was a large mama cat with a grey kitten in one of her pockets. Sitting next to mama cat on the lawn was a puppy, resting in a wicker basket. The floor of Chanel's room was covered with wall-to-wall carpet, a pretty country green with beautiful pink cabbage roses incorporated into the fibers. Her four-poster bed was adorned with a soft pink quilt and a few throw pillows.

Since making choices was not easy for Chanel and usually led to unimaginable frustrations, I only kept two of her favorite toys on top of her toy box. "Hush now," I would whisper softly, and then I attempted to sing her favorite bedtime songs before she went off to sleep. Chanel didn't seem to notice that my singing was off key. As a matter of fact, she kissed my hand and told me I sing beautifully. This Mommy and Chanel time was a joy for both of us. We had a huge bond between us, despite the obstacles. Then, once Chanel was tucked away, I was off to sing to Alonna.

Alonna's room needed to be on the first floor because of her wheelchair. It was at the bottom of the stairs to the left and was the only bedroom on the first floor. Above her bed, (at her request) Armando built some bookshelves that were low enough for her to reach.

Another one of our older daughters moved out of our home to start a new life on the North Shore of Long Island. She moved to a town that was about a 20-minute drive from Patchogue. It's a family-friendly town that hugs the beautiful Long Island Sound. I knew I would miss her help with the girls, as we had taken turns helping each other with the children from time to time.

On June 15, 1995, Armando left for a way over-due trip to

his beautiful homeland, Puerto Rico, to visit his brother Israel Torres in the town of Isabella. I knew his absence was going to be a challenge as it usually took both of us to maintain the rigorous schedules for our two little ones. While he was away, I realized all the little things that he did on a routine bases that I had taken for granted. This reminded me of a large note I saw over one of the desks at work: "You don't realize how much someone does until they stop doing it."

When Armando returned home after a two-week visit, the girls and I were more than happy to see him. I couldn't have imagined facing the arduous tasks and schedules that come along with special needs children without him for one minute longer. As much as we missed him, I was pleased to hear how much Armando enjoyed his trip. He told me that he had seen more of his homeland on this vacation visit then he had in the 25 years he lived there.

On September 3, 1995, we took Chanel to Brookhaven Memorial Hospital as she was complaining of "seeing things upside down" When the medical team examined her, they found she had an irregular apical pulse of 73 yet they could not detect the source. Chanel enjoyed all the attention from the several doctors and nurses that surrounded her for the exam. As she sat fidgeting on the raised examination table, my heart was on edge with her every move in fear she would be kissing the floor at any moment.

"She is charming," one doctor blurts out, "Very charming." We were discharged with instructions to follow up with her pediatrician, and that follow-up visit determined no need for intervention at that time.

CHAPTER SIXTEEN:

CHANEL'S NEW SCHOOL

It was September 1995; Chanel had been discharged from St. Charles Early Intervention Program and was about to begin attending Kindergarten at Medford Avenue Elementary School as part of Patchogue/Medford's Exceptional Student Education program for children with special needs. The classes were small, with only seven or eight students per class, a teacher and a teacher's aide, and at times a volunteer Grandma joined the class to assist the teacher with snack time, singing and reading, as well as providing direct instruction to the children.

This school was much closer than St. Charles in Port Jefferson and now only a ten-minute drive from our home.

On her first day, I drove Chanel to school and had a quick talk with her teacher. I asked that Chanel be placed near the front of the classroom for closer supervision and fewer distractions. We also discussed some of the things that frustrated Chanel.

"She must receive one-step instructions," I informed her teacher. "Chanel is diagnosed with fetal alcohol syndrome and learns better from visual aids and hand over hand instructions. "

"We use the reward system for positive behavior here in my class; we do give one-step instructions and make sure the students fully understand what is expected of them before we go onto the next instruction."

The logical part of my brain was telling me to leave quickly, not for Chanel's sake but for myself. After all, Chanel had already been in a structured school program and was not at all afraid to leave my apron strings. It was me who was feeling apprehensive about leaving her, my head was spinning with worry.

"What if she doesn't sit still?" "What if she hates the class?" "What if she runs off and gets lost in the chaos at the end of the day?" I didn't think her teacher was prepared for all the behavior issues that go along with fetal alcohol syndrome, and I didn't want to overwhelm her with all my instructions on the first day of class. After some final reassurance that Chanel would be walked to the bus and seated by an assistant before the other students were dismissed, I quickly gave Chanel a kiss on her forehead and walked off briskly.

I looked forward to reading all the notes Chanel's teacher put in her backpack each day. On the first day she wrote:

Welcome to Medford Elementary School. We are happy you are part of our ESE program and look forward to providing a year filled with rewarding experiences for your child. Chanel had a fun day; however I now know why you requested she sit right up front. Chanel definitely does need extra supervision. She left the group several times and preferred to be with the adults i.e., volunteer Grandma and teacher's aide. I look forward to our Parent-Teachers meeting to discuss any further advice or strategies that you may want to share with me. All information will be helpful in meeting Chanel's special needs.

A few months or so into Chanel's kindergarten year we were invited to Chanel's school for a play she would take part in. My camcorder was charged and ready to go. I really enjoyed being with her. It was interesting to watch her lack of interaction with the other students. As they were playing together or chatting in clusters, Chanel remained off to the side.

When the school principal walked into the class, Chanel ran to him and jumped into his lap, lovingly stroking his arm and head. I wasn't at all comfortable with this petting, and I could see from the principal's reaction that he was uncomfortable as well. Even though he removed her from his lap several times, Chanel was unable to interpret social cues from others and climbed up in his lap again. I noticed her being inappropriately affectionate with adults on a few other occasions. The principal squirmed to get Chanel off his lap, but Chanel did not comprehend appropriate touch and boundaries. Eventually the principal jumped up and walked over to speak with the teacher's aide. When I discussed my concerns about Chanel's behavior with the teacher, I asked how often the principal came into the class. "This is the first time they met" she whispered to me. We summoned Chanel over to where we were standing and attempted to distract her from tugging on the principal's suit jacket. I often wondered what the principal and the teacher said after we left the class. Boy, I would have loved to be a fly on the wall for that conference.

Throughout the rest of the year we received notes from Chanel's teacher. Almost all the notes made mention of the adorable dresses she wore to class, her endearing personality and sometimes her tendency to become overly affectionate. Then there were the comments and concerns about Chanel's inability to focus or sit still, her short attention span and impulsiveness. Of course it was nothing I didn't already know about. I worked very closely with her teacher and loved our open communication and strong parent-teacher relationship.

On March 7, 1996, Armando and I became re-certified as foster parents. Can you believe we were ready to take on more foster children? And they arrived for the next several years. One after the next we were given a list of their special needs as Ar-

Sondra and Armando

mando and I tended to our family and our new foster children as best we could, and loved every minute of it. Some came with very heart breaking stories that would follow them throughout life. Many left our home, but never left our hearts. Grazina and Christina were especially dear to us. I think of them often and would love to reunite with them at some point, along with many of the other foster children that stayed with us over the years.

On June 14, 1996, another school year had passed, and I was excited to attend Chanel's end of school year play. My trusty little camcorder was once again ready to go. I had that song stuck in my head: "Fish are swimming in the ocean, they are causing such commotion, grab a paddle, grab a pail, WE'LL SET OUR SIGHTS ON THE BIGGEST WHALE!" On the drive home Chanel and I competed to see who could sing the loudest, luckily we had our windows closed.

I just loved this little girl, who was so exuberant and full of life, always happy and ready to share a hug.

On August 28, 1996, it was time for another daughter and helper to leave the nest. The Torres family gathered to celebrate her departure with many of our neighbors, friends and co-workers joining us for the send-off. Gail and Dale, our next-door neighbors, led some of the party goers out back where the music got louder and, the friendly chit-chat began.

Chanel was making her usual rounds, asking for hugs and kisses from almost everyone whether she knew them or not. She was extremely hyperactive that day, tripping over things more than usual, falling while going up the stairs and when coming back down. My eyes were feeling like slinkies. She had already dropped her plate of food and two glasses of juice. I was afraid she would get hurt. She didn't seem to be able to focus on what was going on around her.

She was still talking to her imaginary friends, GeaGea, Petey and Margaret, even though the doctor said this would stop by age five or six. I noticed she talked to them when she was off to the side by herself or in her room alone. She must have known this behavior was not acceptable.

Chanel continued to need constant monitoring and supervision, just like the pre-school teacher informed me a few years back. Luckily, my neighbors all knew Chanel's diagnosis of fetal alcohol syndrome. They were all understanding and a tremendous help.

From time to time I thought about Christine, Chanel's birth mother. Where was she, what was she up to, did she still live in Islip? Had she been thinking about Chanel? I would have loved to show her what a beautiful young lady Chanel was becoming. However, she was also becoming more impulsive and fearless. She didn't think about the consequences and never learned from her past experiences. She jumped off the sofa head first onto our hard wood floors, or climbed to the top of a bookshelf or ran into the street without looking. My admonishments were completely ignored as she repeated the same behaviors even if the behavior led to her getting seriously hurt.

After a near miss when I heard a car come to a screeching halt and a neighbor yelling for Chanel to get out of the street, we restricted Chanel to the backyard. Armando fenced in the yard and set up a swing-set, a play kitchen and lots of riding toys for the girls.

Armando and Jessica left to visit family in North Carolina. Once there was a time I didn't mind flying at all. In fact, I have flown more than a dozen times, to and from Puerto Rico, and back and forth from New York to Florida. I'm not sure what happened but suddenly I became overwhelmed with the fear of flying. "C'mon Mom," my daughters would prod me, "Get over this fear of flying. They have therapy for that, you know."

Once again I found myself alone with the girls, which proved to be a huge challenge for me. Armando was only gone a few days this time, but it felt like forever.

Chanel was still wearing diapers at night and played a game while I tried to change her diaper. Sporting her birthday suit, she called out, "CATCH ME IF YOU CAN, MOMMY!"

I couldn't help but laugh as I ran after her, almost as uncoordinated as she was as I attempted to snatch her up while she darted out of my reach. This was a game that Armando usually took pleasure in. He told me the running kept him in shape.

One night, soon after I snagged her little body and placed her in the bathtub, I excitedly told her, "I have a surprise for you downstairs." While she was sleeping I baked some chocolate chip cookies, about three dozen for the family. Chanel hesitantly helped dry off and dawdled as I helped her to get dressed. I was perplexed as to her behavior, because usually when she heard the word "cookies" she couldn't get there fast enough. Why was she purposefully stalling us from getting downstairs? It didn't take long before I found out why, the cookie jar was just about empty. "Chanel, do you know where the cookies are?" Of course, she denied taking them. Since Alonna couldn't reach that middle shelf from her wheelchair, it was pretty obvious who had taken them.

We had many talks with Chanel about taking things that didn't belong to her or taking things without permission.

Her denials were so realistic and emphatic, as she pleaded to avoid any punishment or consequences, "I didn't do it, Mommy, please believe me, it wasn't me, I SWEAR!" The week before, when my small radio and handheld game went missing, I had heard the same heart-wrenching pleas and with extreme expression:" I DIDN'T DO IT MOMMY, PLEASE BELIEVE ME; IT WASN'T ME, I SWEAR!"

Armando and Jessica returned from North Carolina with lots of family pictures and videos. You have no idea how happy I was to have Armando back home.

In October 1996, I received a call from Chanel's teacher expressing her concerns. "Chanel is so very hyperactive and impulsive in class, she doesn't think before doing things, we're afraid she will get hurt. She can't focus on what's going on around her. Her attention span is almost nonexistent. She's having a lot of difficulty with numbers. She can't add 1+1, the basic rudimentary math. At times we give her color cards and ask her to point out a particular color and she is able to correctly point out the blue card, green card, etc., but then the next day she doesn't have a clue what color the card is."

At home I worked diligently with Chanel, reading to her almost nightly, and working with the flash cards, numbers and colors. Sometimes I felt like I was making progress, but then soon after the progress evaporated. It helped when a friend reminded me that memory is a large component of cognition and plays an important role in development. So it was understandable that Chanel's memory impairment, caused by the fetal alcohol syndrome, was having a negative effect on the development of her social skills as well as dampening her academic performance, especially in mathematics.

On October 30, 1996, I made a decision that I regret to this day. At this point I had been hearing just about every day that the school therapists were all concerned Chanel might get hurt. I wanted to try different behavior modification techniques first, but at the encouragement of the doctor, in fact a team of specialists at one of our local hospitals, I allowed Chanel to start a regimen of the drug Ritalin. I read the side effects of this drug, and saw that some of them were pretty serious. Her first dose was given with great hesitation, and made her very tired. On Ritalin, she often slept during the day, in class, on the bus and whenever else she got a chance. The dose was very low. Though the sleepiness happened immediately, the therapeutic effect didn't kick in until three weeks after her initial dose. I also noticed weight loss, something Chanel couldn't afford. I tried feeding her small amounts of food more frequently, made healthy high calorie milk shakes, sat with her at meal times to encourage her to eat more, but all of these attempts failed to counter the weight loss.

On January 16, 1997, Chanel saw Dr. Water, a psychiatrist. He discontinued the time-released Ritalin and gave us a script for immediate release Ritalin. The new immediate release Ritalin took effect quickly with no wait time. The school nurse administered the medication to her so the desired effect lasted for a good portion of her school day. Weeks went by, and then months, with no more daily reports from teacher's worrying about her getting hurt. I was starting to hope Ritalin would be the magic pill for ALL behavior issues, but that wasn't the case. There were still a few problematic areas and occasional concerns from her teachers. Chanel became easily frustrated because she wanted so much to please and couldn't always because of her limitations. For example, her fine and gross motor skills were weak, making it difficult for her to write. Her academic grades were a few years behind, but Chanel tried her very best.

On March 20, 1997, I walked into Chanel's classroom at 9:00 a.m., and sat at a table with her teacher. Chanel was off to the side, sitting alone while the other children played in a cluster. It was obvious she didn't have the best social skills and not even one close friend.

"Chanel is a pleasure to have in class," the teacher proceeded to tell me, and I just love the cute dresses she wears. But I do have some concerns about the tremors in her hands. She is academically two to three years behind in most areas, though she does do better with reading then in other academic areas."

The teacher also mentioned Chanel's speech deficits and a few other concerns, but there was no mention of hyperactivity. The immediate release Ritalin was working.

"She seems to be able to focus for a longer period of time, much better than in the past." The teacher continued.

"This is progress," I think to myself. Baby steps but progress nonetheless.

Ritalin had no effect on the stories Chanel made up. Luckily, she had never been a skilled fibber and it was always easy to know when she was fibbing. The more I learned through my research of fetal alcohol syndrome, the more concerned I became. I read that as fetal alcohol syndrome children get older they become more successful and better at concealing their fibs. Would that happen with Chanel? Even now she sometimes mixes part truths with her imagination in hopes of being more believable. What I was still at a loss for was the reason behind these made-up stories. She was having difficulty distinguishing between reality and fantasy. In most cases children fib to cover up their actions and the consequences that come from their actions. Yet Chanel's fibs were so benign and had no real basis behind them. For example, once Chanel came to me and told me she had been on a school trip and I hadn't signed a permission slip. Her teacher confirmed that Chanel had made the whole thing up. But why? I had to try to stay ahead of her fibbing and thoroughly investigate whatever she told me.

On April 8, 1997, there was an accident at school that sent Chanel to Brookhaven Memorial Hospital. Another student had been running with his mouth open and collided with Chanel. His teeth embedded into the side of Chanel's face near her right eye area, she received 6 sutures. I hated when she got hurt. Having a daughter with fetal alcohol syndrome, I was always on heightened alert, waiting for that emergency phone call. While the teacher said the accident wasn't Chanel's fault, I wondered what she could have done differently to prevent it. Another child may have perceived that the student was coming towards them, and moved out of the way, but Chanel may not have noticed. She often played by herself, off to the side from the other children and oblivious to what they were doing. Children with fetal alcohol syndrome may appear to be capable of much more than they can deliver, as is the case with Chanel.

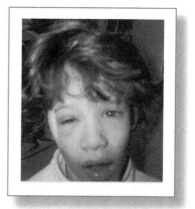

Picture taken after a student ran into Chanel and his teeth embedded into the side of her right eye area

CHAPTER SEVENTEEN:

HERE WE GO AGAIN
BABY REANNA

In May 1998, a foster care placement worker called and asked if I would take in baby Reanna, who was in the hospital. He proceeded to tell me this was a very sick little girl, she needed open heart surgery, she was blind and deaf, and might not live for more than five or six months. I gasped my reply "I must talk to my husband before I can give you an answer. I have a feeling he will pass on this one." Just as I thought, Armando quietly told me he could not handle a baby dying in his home. Off I went to check on Chanel and Alonna. While I respected Armando's decision, I couldn't get baby Reanna out of my head. The next morning when Armando left for work, I raced to the phone and called the placement worker. I asked if I could visit the baby.

"Of course," he said, "just talk to the charge nurse, tell her I sent you there to visit with baby Reanna." Shaking and somewhat

113

nervous, I gathered up my things, put my grandson BoDean in the car and off to the hospital we went. After wandering around the 11th floor for few minutes, I finally stopped a woman and asked her where I could find the charge nurse.

She replied, "That would be me, how can I help you?"

I disclosed to her that I was a prospective foster mother for little Reanna, and that the foster care placement worker had sent me here to visit with her. The nurse guided me to baby Reanna's room and left us there alone for a quiet visit. Reanna was in a small clear plastic carrier, hooked up to an IV, while a nasogastric tube was pumping formula into her tiny body. I walked over to her, finding myself choked up, trying my best to control my tears. Here was this tiny baby girl, almost two-and-a half months old with her eyes shut and somewhat sunken. She didn't seem to be aware of my presence as she rested quietly. I clapped my hands fairly loudly, but she didn't startle. The cardiac monitor wires were attached to her tiny little chest, while the machines emitted a soft and rhythmic "Beep, beep, beep." She was neatly wrapped up like a little taco from a local restaurant. I gently stroked her hand, then her little forehead, all while she remained expression-less. After a few minutes of attempting to get a reaction from her, I sat in the large plastic-covered chair next to where she was resting.

My mind was racing with fleeting ideas. "Why couldn't we foster this baby? Even if she dies in our home, at least she would be surrounded by people that love her" Just as my thoughts were about to get carried away even more, a woman walked in and headed right for the baby. I wasn't sure who she was, but she briskly walked over to baby Reanna and stroked her little hands and her forehead just as I had done. I wondered if this was a social worker or someone from the foster care placement unit, I was wrong.

After the woman plopped herself in a chair adjacent to mine, I peeked over at her as she sat sullenly and somewhat slumped over.

"Do you work here?" I asked.

"No, no, I'm Reanna's mother," she replied.

I didn't know how to react or how to respond.

"Who are you?" she whispered to me. Now, I was nervous. What should I tell her? Should I be honest and tell her I am contemplating on becoming Reanna's foster mom or make up some story like, "I was passing by and saw your baby, and I just wanted to come peek in on her" Of course I told her the truth, "Suffolk County Department of Social Services-foster care placement department has sent me here to visit your baby." I went on to tell her how pretty her baby was. The woman started to cry and then stormed out of the room. I felt so bad; I assumed she would have known her baby was going into foster care. I heard a loud commotion in the hall, as Reanna's mother, Tammy, yelled and carried on. The charge nurse told Tammy that CPS would contact her, and that her baby must go into foster care. Despite their attempts to calm Tammy down, she continued to wail loudly.

The security guard walked over and told her, "If you cannot control your emotions then you will be escorted out of the building. You are disrupting the other families." Then she come back into Reanna's room, sat adjacent to me once again and began to talk.

"They took my other baby away, they can't take this one away. Why, WHY, are they doing this to me?"

"Listen, Tammy," I said softly, I have been a foster mom for many years and often parents who have had their child removed from their care are given a plan to follow, in order to regain custody of their child. If you comply with CPS requests, your baby will come home to you" As I looked directly at her, Tammy seemed to relax a bit, cupping her hands over her face as she cried quietly. I wasn't sure if I should hug her or what, so I patted her on her hand. I wanted to comfort her in some way. "Tammy if my husband and I do take your baby as our foster child, Reanna would be in good hands, and we could work together. I am open to phone calls. You could call my home and check in on your baby whenever you wanted to."

Once I returned home, I really had my work cut out for me. I had to convince Armando that we must give this baby a chance. I rehashed in my head over and over again how I would accomplish this.

Raising a child with special needs is always a work in progress, with lots of unexpected hairpin twists, turns and blind convoluted roads. Our days were always full of surprises. We never knew what to expect from day to day. Armando and I had always been committed to being the best adoptive parents ever, and we made a promise when we signed those adoption papers that we would take excellent care our children. Would we be spreading ourselves too thin by taking in another special needs child? Raising one child with special needs is a two-person full-time job, and we already had two. Just as my mind was running wild with these thoughts, I snapped back to reality as Armando walked in the back door. He appeared tired and wanted to take a shower.

"WAIT, wait a minute," I called out to him, "I have something to tell you."

"Okay, where is she?" he replied.

"Where's who? " I asked.

"The baby, where's the baby?" Now does he know me, or what?

"Oh my goodness, Armando, I would never take a foster child in without talking it over with you first, BUT I did go see her. I want to ask you again if we could please, PLEASE take this baby in."

He just couldn't handle a baby dying in our home, he said, then after a minute he looked at me and continued, "Okay I'll tell you what, if you go and tell the girls that we are taking in a baby that's going to die and if they say it's okay, then I'll be okay with it." I can still hear his voice, with his Spanish accent. I knew just what Armando was thinking, "the girls will surely say no."

I gathered all the girls into Alonna's bedroom, and started carefully, "Listen, I have something to ask you. What do you think about us taking in another foster baby?" Before I could get to the important details, they all started yelling loudly, "Yes, yes, yes, yes!"

"Give me a chance to tell you the rest, I said, "This is a very sick little baby. There is a good chance that she will die in a few months, and God will come and take her. He has a bed ready and waiting for her."

None of this seemed to matter to the girls, they continued to yell "Yes, yes, yes, yes!" I wasn't convinced that they truly understood what I was saying. From their questions, I got the sense that they thought death was both temporary and reversible.

I tried explaining again, "Dying is forever. If she dies she won't ever be able to come back. But at least she will be with family that will love her until that time." Meanwhile, Armando was just outside the bedroom door and heard the full conversation. As he nodded his head with approval, he said "But we are NOT adopting her, we have enough!" he sighed with a smirk like smile.

It was May 14, 1998 when I arrived at the hospital to pick up little Reanna, Tammy was already in the room. Two nurses were removing the wires from Reanna's little chest and the nasogastric tube from her nose. The IV's had already been removed. After a quick diaper change, they handed me some paper work to sign and told me to bring my car right up to the front door and then return to the room. I did as they requested. As I got out of the elevator on my way back from the parking area, I heard a commotion as Tammy cried out, "Please don't take my baby PEEEELEASE! A nurse and a security guard brought the baby and her belongings to me, and then escorted me to my car as I held the baby tightly. The second security guard stayed with Tammy in Reanna's empty room. I drove straight to my daughter Jessica's house and I started crying as I pulled into her driveway.

"Oh my goodness," I blurted out, "I feel like I just kidnapped someone's baby!"

Jessica attempted to console me by reminding me that if it wasn't me that fostered this baby, someone else would have.

"Obviously CPS had a good reason for putting the baby in foster care," she added. Jessica was always very supportive of us fostering children and this day was no different.

When I returned home with this new little baby, Chanel was very curious, asking me all sorts of questions. "Does her mommy know you took her baby?" "Will she see her mommy again?"

I carefully answered all her questions. Chanel ran to tell Alonna, "The baby is here, hurry, come look!" Chanel offered to help me put the baby's belongings in Armando's and my bedroom, right next to the bassinet. Chanel and Alonna were doing a wonderful job of welcoming this little one into our family.

In July and August of 1998, the Torres family vacationed in Florida for a family reunion, when the Morgan family finally got to meet Reanna and Alonna for the first time. This was a very challenging vacation. Reanna was a good baby and didn't cry very much, and Alonna was easy to please and was

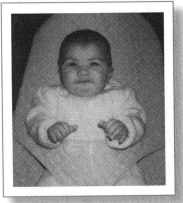

Reanna (Rosina)

very pleasant to be around. She loved to entertain everyone with her wheel chair pop-a-wheelies.

Traveling with Chanel, however, was another story. Because of her impulsive issues, she needed constant one-on-one supervision and guidance. Some thought I overdid it, but my experiences with Chanel taught me that any less supervision could be disastrous for her.

Early in the morning on August 3rd, our last day in Florida, my sister Jorain asked me "What's wrong with Chanel, the left side of her face is droopy."

Even though I didn't see the drooping personally and she seemed to be fine, I immediately called and left a message with her doctor in New York. Chanel denied any complaints and was playing around as she always did. "We should be heading back to New York in a few hours. We can have her checked out there, I decided." When her doctor finally returned my call, I requested Chanel be taken off the Ritalin. Her doctor agreed and we made a plan of care. We scheduled appointments for Chanel to see the neurologist and the behavior specialist in two days. That would be the last day she would ever take Ritalin again.

On, August 5, 1998, Chanel was taken to the hospital for an MRI. The results showed no transient ischemic attacks (mini strokes) as I feared from her symptom of facial drooping. I made up my mind that I would never allow myself to be coaxed into putting her on that stuff again.

As we unpacked our suitcases from our Florida vacation I found a ton of "HOUSE FOR SALE" books in Armando's suitcase. He circled a few homes in St. Petersburg, Florida, pointing to a few really nice ones with four to five bedrooms. Five bedrooms, I think? All of our older daughters have left the nest;

we only had Chanel and Alonna and our little foster daughter Reanna. Armando had said we weren't going to adopt again. Our plan was to sell our home in Patchogue, NY in about one to two years and then move to Florida.

Here we go again, I was so madly in love with little Reanna and I watched Armando smiling at her in a special way. He didn't even realize it but he was becoming attached to her as well. She was pretty stable with her cardiac status at this time, although she still needed surgery to repair her heart defect [Tetralogy of Fallot].

For the rest of this year Armando and I did our best to keep Chanel safe. At times it seemed like there was always a nightmare about to happen. We were constantly on edge with anticipation. While I stayed adamant about "NO MORE RITALIN," the next few months proved to be very challenging. My nerves were fried beyond belief! Her impulsivity had increased to the point that whenever she moved I gasped for fear she would get hurt. In one month alone, she innocently broke a few dishes, the light switch, the TV control, the towel bar in the bathroom, my radio dial and the list continued. Whenever she met resistance she didn't stop to ask for help, she just used force and she was much stronger than she looked! For example, if the fan was already at the highest speed, but she wanted to turn it up even higher, she just turned the knob until it snapped off. If her towel got caught while she was pulling it off the rack, she yanked on it until the screws came right out of the wall. She apologized sincerely after each incident.

One of the things I loved most about Chanel was her ability to make people smile. At night, Alonna and Chanel whispered secrets and chuckled together. I think they were talking about boys. I was witnessing beautiful young girls with sparkling eyes emerge. Chanel was right there for Alonna, ready to protect her from any bullies at school, and the first to defend her against anyone who might make fun of her disability or her wheelchair. Chanel did not tolerate bullying at all, and would protect anyone who was being victimized. Chanel herself had been bullied for her stuttering. I was starting to see a great future for her as an advocate, if we could only get her past the impulse urges!

On January 28th, 1999, the temperature was in the low 30's. Reanna had her first open heart surgery at North Shore University Hospital in Manhasset, NY, for repair of her ventricular septal defect (an opening in the wall of the heart). Our own hearts were truly broken into dusty little pieces for this precious baby girl. Armando and I were right by her side on surgery day, even though as foster parents we had no legal input in her care. That really bothered me! Our neighbor and friend Eileen stayed at home with the other two girls. Chanel often appeared more mature and capable than she actually was and we learned from experience that it was best not to leave her with a sitter for more than an hour or two. So during Reanna's recovery in the cardiovascular intensive care unit, Armando and I took turns driving the 45-50 minutes to the hospital so one of us could always be at home.

Over the next few months Chanel's behavior continued as before. She was still talking to her imaginary friends, Petey, Gea-Gea and Margaret. She also continued to tell fibs. One day she told me she saw our neighbor Ruth in her yard, gardening. Then, I discovered Ruth left town the week before for a month-long trip. I always confronted Chanel when she fibbed, and told her that I knew she made up the story. Sometimes she denied that they were made up and other times she apologized.

On May 5, 2000, we had a déjà vu day. It was 8:00 a.m. and we were once again at the Cohalan Court Complex in Islip because at 9:00 a.m., we would adopt Reanna and she would become Rosina Torres. We named her after my mother who encouraged the adoption. There we sat in the judge's chambers: Athena, who was the adoption case worker; our friends, Krissy and Garret; our daughters, Chanel, Alonna, Jessica and Dana; as well as our lawyer and of course Armando and I. The room felt very familiar, and the procedure was the same as it had been for Alonna and Chanel.

In closed chambers for Rosina's adoption.

Rosina's adoption

Rosina was dressed in a very flamboyant pink and white beaded dress with a puffy tutu-like bodice. Her hair was fixed just so, and her new shoes and socks were perfect. As soon as Armando and I signed many papers the judge proclaimed, "Armando and Sondra Torres, you are now the parents of Rosina Torres."

Chanel jumped up with joy and yelled out "YES" and laughter ensued. Armando's eyes were lit up with joy, as he had become very attached to this beautiful baby girl.

I wanted to call Rosina's birth mother Tammy, to share the wonderful news. She had appeared in court a few months back to sign the papers that freed Reanna for adoption to the Torres family. I had given her our phone number and home address. Tammy never did contact us and I had no way to reach her.

Despite the severity of her many birth defects; Rosina had already outlived her doctor's predictions. She was neither deaf nor blind. She still showed no response when I clapped my hands near her ears or waved my hand close to her eyes, which the doctor explained "could be the result of being deprived of attention from her birth mother during those critical first few days of life."

The next few months proved to be very challenging, with most of the attention being spent on little Rosina, Chanel was doing her best to behave. Rosina was taken to the hospital several times, often via ambulance, sometimes as often as two or three times a week. Chanel was not sure what to make of this new little one and all the attention she required. Sometimes the over stimulation was too much for Chanel to bear and she would retreat to her room with her friends, Gea-Gea, Petey, and Margaret.

In June 2000, Armando and I decided to hire a housekeeper so we could spend more time with the girls. It proved to be the best decision ever. Even though, I had to incorporate the additional cost of the housekeeping service into our usual budget; I was more than willing to cut back on other spending. I loved having the extra time to spend with my family, as I was still working the 11:00 p.m. to 7:00 a.m. shift as charge nurse at a Health Care Facility.

Our first interview was with two male housekeepers. Their sales pitch worked right away, and sure enough they proved to be very good at what they did and even taught me a few tricks. As time passed, I had no complaints about their ability to follow directions. What was a concern was Chanel's fascination with two new men in our home. She was always the first to greet them at the door with a big hug. These hugs made me very uncomfortable and were unprovoked by the men. I had a long, talk with Chanel and explained the difference between appropriate and inappropriate hugs. She complied for a week or so, but it was what I noticed next that really frightened me. Not only was Chanel stretching up her arms for these hugs, the older man seemed to be enjoying them a little too much. Through my peripheral vision I saw a smirk from the older man as he hugged Chanel back. Chanel was an overly affectionate ten-and-a-half- year-old girl who preferred to be with adults over children her own age. It wasn't a hard decision to make, the men had to go!

As we started the search for a new cleaning team, we knew that this time we would hire woman housekeepers. It didn't take long. After a few months we found the perfect team of two women I knew from school. Once again I had extra time to do fun things with my family.

On June 7, 2000, Rosina got to talk to her birth mother, Tammy on the phone. Chanel was fascinated by this phone call and inquired about her own birth mother, Christine. I knew that this day would come at some point.

She asked all the predictable questions. "Where does Christine live?" "Does she work?" "What does she look like?" "Do I have any brothers or sisters?"

I sat Chanel down in a quiet room so we could chat, patiently answering all of her questions. "You do have a sister, her name is Susan. I don't know who she is or where she lives, but she loves animals and wants to be a veterinarian when she grows up. As far as your birth mother Christine, I have lost contact with her, what I do know is that Christine loved you very much and signed the adoption papers to give you a better chance at life." Just as abruptly as the subject came up, the questions stopped.

One thing Armando and I did as often as possible was to vacation with the girls, even if it was a vacation to nowhere. On July 20, 2000 we had a very specific vacation planned. First we traveled to Fort Bragg in North Carolina, to satisfy Chanel's curiosity about the base. Our van was packed with lots of supplies for the children. We sang silly songs with the girls all the way to North Carolina; a family member took us on a tour through the barracks and around the town. Chanel was very curious and asked lots of questions, pointing to the camouflaged jeeps and the helicopter, wanting to hear all about what they were used for. After the brief tour we were off again to Florida via I95 for a family reunion and Rosina's adoption party. The rest of my family was meeting us in Holiday, Florida, for Rosina's adoption celebration.

We arrived at our Tahitian resort hotel in Holiday, on July 23,

2000 at 3:00 p.m. and checked into room # 138. Members of the Morgan family would be traveling from the Miami area in the next few days. Several rooms to the right and left of us were reserved for them. In the meantime we enjoyed the Florida weather, and did lots of shopping and sightseeing with the girls. In the evenings we played in the very large beautiful heated swimming pool. As family started to arrive, some of them meeting our girls for the first time, they gathered in our hotel room so we could get caught up on the family chit chat.

Rosina's adoption dinner party was on July 29, 2000. She was wearing the very same fancy pink dress she wore to the Islip court-house on adoption day. We were all in party mode, as one-by-one our guests arrived: my mother, sister Jorain and her friend Barbara, my niece Lisa, her husband Bill and their son Billy, my daughter Jessica and her Husband Joe and their family, my daughter Trudy and her family, Trudy's in-laws Marta and Juan Carlos and grandparents in-laws Suzanna and German, Carlos' brother Roberto, my sister Rosina and her daughter Vanessa, my God-daughter Elizabeth and her husband Wolf and their family, Linda and her husband, daughter Brendalyn and a few other friends.

While Rosina was all smiles, Chanel was fascinated with all the family that was in one room. Alonna was being very quiet and taking it all in. After our guests left, Armando and I asked the girls to sit down on the bed in our hotel room because we had an announcement to make. "Before heading back to New York we are going to stop off at Disney World for a few days of fun to complete the adoption celebration." Alonna and Chanel were so excited they screamed for almost 15 minutes straight, my ears didn't stop ringing for several hours. Rosina was too young to understand what Disney World was all about, until we arrived on August 1, 2000 and she spotted Mickey Mouse. She recognized him right away. Armando and I got a healthy dose of hugs and kisses from all the girls. This was truly a vacation we would never forget.

In September, 2000, Armando and I signed Chanel up for swimming lesions. "The best way to overcome the fear of swimming is to face your fears head on" Armando said. What fears? Chanel didn't have ANY fears! We did come to the conclusion that, swimming could be an excellent outlet for releasing some of Chanel's bottled up energy. September 23, 2000 was her first day at the YMCA. Armando drove her and stayed with her during these sessions. The lessons did tire her out, somewhat. Each day Chanel put her bathing suit on and pranced around the house like a princess. Knocking things off the table as she spun around, once falling right into a china cabinet with glass doors, luckily the glass didn't shatter.

On October 4th, the last day of her lessons, she showed Armando and I all the neat swimming tricks she had learned. Excitedly yelling out "LOOK, LOOK, I CAN SWIM, I CAN SWIM"

"Great," I thought, "Now I have to worry about her being overconfident while swimming."

NOTE TO CHRISTINE FROM CHANEL:

OCTBER 2000

DEAR CHRISTINE

My name is Chanel now. I don't if you know this. Sometimes I have trouble thinking in school and at home. My hands shack and I have a hard time speling. I hope I get to vesit you one day I have a lot I want to Talk to you about. I hope that you are ok. I want to know why you gave me up. Do I have sisters and brothers. What are you doing with your life? Are you married? I have good life now.

Why can't I think right. I have 7 sisters and some foster sisters. Alonna and I are best sister friends. We have a lot of animals. I want to become a vet when I grow up and talke care of lots of animals. I don't remember what you look like I do want t meet you one day. I love to read I am very good at it but I do like I have to share my books wath Alonna. What colar is your hair? Do you live in ny? Where do you work?

I will write you again Chanel

At this point, I had still not shown Chanel any of the letters and notes that Christine sent home in the baby bag with her after their visits a few years back. They were in a safe place and someday we would go through them together.

By December 2000, Rosina's seizures, which had been happening for a year or so, were becoming more frequent. What I did notice was Chanel's amazing ability to put her fetal alcohol syndrome on the back burner, stepping up to help organize things when our family was having a crisis. She was always the first on the scene to help. She helped make phone calls to 911, she locked up the pets, and she waved down the paramedics, allowing me to stay right at Rosina's side. She also made sure someone got the baby bag ready, along with a face sheet with all Rosina's medical information on it for the ER doctors. This was a trick I learned from being a nurse for so many years.

On December 2, 2000, Rosina had a grand mal seizure and was off to the hospital AGAIN. The paramedics knew her well by this point. Doctors had labeled her seizures as atypical febrile seizures since she seized with just slight elevations in temperatures. There were times when she had two to three seizures in a 24-hour period and had even coded during two of her seizures.

On December 31, 2000, we celebrated Chanel and Alonna's birthdays. Alonna's actual birthday was on January 9th, but we celebrated them together. Chanel was now 11 years old and Alonna was 12 years old. We had a quiet dinner at home followed by cake and milk with other family members, when the girls opened up their requested gifts. A few of our neighbors also came by with gifts and birthday cheer.

CHAPTER EIGHTEEN:

A TRAUMATIC EVENT IN CHANEL'S LIFE

On June 20, 2001, my cousin Linda from Rochester, NY came to stay with us for a few weeks. This was a treat beyond belief. We talked into the late hours of the night and took long walks around the neighborhood. We shared personal stories from the past and present. I enjoyed her company immensely and we made an everlasting connection.

During Linda's visit, Chanel and our family were invited to a very special moving up ceremony. Linda, Chanel and I attended the breezy outdoor event. Both, Linda and I waited with anticipation for

Aunt Linda & Chanel

Chanel's name to be called out. Finally, the announcer called her name "Chanel Torres". As Chanel walked up to receive her award, Linda and I loudly applauded her great achievement. Her award was for the most improved student at Tremont Elementary School. We were so very proud of her, as she had struggled with behavior issues her whole life. I think she was beginning to recognize what triggered her poor choices and bad behavior, and it was obviously leading to better results.

On July 5, 2001, just before Linda went back home to upstate New York, we did some shopping at a local department store where she treated me to a beautiful blouse. When we returned home, Chanel was jumping up and down with excitement after receiving a phone call from her Teacher's aide, Mrs. Dee. This was the second year Chanel was assigned to her class, and she knew Chanel almost as well as we did. She called to invite Chanel for a visit at her house. I hesitated, since I wasn't comfortable letting Chanel out of our sight. Yet I knew that Chanel really needed to experience time away from home and this seemed like a good opportunity. She was eleven and a half years old now and in need of some friends. I talked to Mrs. Dee and got all the right answers to my questions: no they didn't live near a highway, no there wasn't a swimming pool, yes there would be plenty of supervision with one adult for three children. I decided to let Chanel visit, requesting that the visit be limited to two hours.

At 3:45 p.m. Mrs. Dee pulled up to collect Chanel. We talked for about ten minutes and off they went with the promise that Chanel would be dropped off at home at 6:00 p.m. As I was doing the dishes, Chanel called me from Mrs. Dee's and was in a very joyful mood. She asked if she could stay until 7:00 p.m. because they were about to sit down and eat a spaghetti dinner. After talking to Mrs. Dee I agreed she could stay until 7:00 p.m. but no later. As it was I was nervous; this was the longest she had been away from me other than during school hours.

At 6:50 p.m., there was a knock on the door, a loud knock, full of purpose and urgency. When I opened the door, I first saw Mrs. Dee standing there with a frightened look upon her face. Then I looked down at Chanel and wondered why they were knocking, why didn't they just walk in? It was at this moment I noticed the white towel held up to Chanel's face, saturated with blood! I started to scream out, "Oh my God, what happenned? WHAT HAPPENED?"

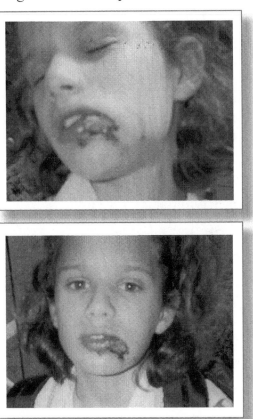

Mrs. Dee was begging me to calm down, but I was beyond reassurance.

"Remove the towel!" I firmly told Chanel. She looked so frightened, her eyes were huge and her frail little body was shaking. The towel was soaked with blood as it dripped all down Chanel's clothing and onto the front steps.

"The dog bit me, Mommy, the dog did it." Chanel cried out in her very weak and garbled voice. I was so horrified at what I was seeing and I yelled out to Mrs. Dee, "WHAT DOG? Why didn't you call the paramedics or just take Chanel to the emergency room?"

Her reply just floored me. "Well, when I was younger, my mother took a child to the emergency room because the boy got hurt, but the doctor wouldn't do anything for the child because the mother wasn't there to sign the consent forms"

Shaking my head in disbelief, I grabbed Chanel by the hand and put her in my car as I drove at the top of the speed limit to the hospital. The ER was crowded that day. I cut to the front of the triage line and walked up to the nurse. I nervously explained to her that my daughter was just attacked by a pit bull. She proceeded to tell me I would have to go to the end of the line.

"No way!" I shouted, "I'm taking her to another hospital!" As we raced towards the exit, the nurse called out at me "I'm going to report you to CPS. Once you sign your daughter in, you must leave her here for treatment."

I pointed to the other people waiting in line and said, "None of these people are in dire distress. This is a true emergency and there is no time to waste. She needs treatment NOW!"

While the nurse tried to convince me to stay, I stormed out the door and headed for the next hospital about 15-20 minutes away. As I was driving away I realized that I had never signed Chanel in, so that triage nurse didn't even know our names and couldn't report us to CPS. When we arrived at the next hospital, much to our surprise this waiting room was even fuller than the last. I walked up to the triage nurse and asked Chanel to remove the towel from her face. As soon as the nurse saw that a large part of Chanel's lip and face were missing she guided us to a treatment room immediately. When I told her what had happened at the previous hospital, the nurse patted me on the shoulder and said "You did the right thing; this isn't something that can wait."

Mrs. Dee followed us to the first hospital then off to the second hospital. I was so angry at her, I didn't even want to look at her, let alone have her trailing right behind my every move!

Chanel received over 50 sutures to her mouth and face with only a local anesthetic. She was a trooper and cried very little. While we waited for another doctor to check Chanel out, I asked Mrs. Dee, "What happened?"

She proceeded to tell me, "Our dumb dog already bit my son on his hand, bit my husband on his foot and now Chanel." The tragedy all unfolded when Chanel bent down to pet the dog on the head while carrying a plate of spaghetti. "Don't worry, he had all his shots," she continued, "We take him to the vet over on Medford Avenue."

You can be sure that from that point on, whenever Chanel was invited to visit someone, I added another question to my list, "Do you have a dog, and is he safe around children?"

It was late at night when we arrived home from this horrific mess. A police officer arrived shortly after we did to take Chanel's report. I did my best to comfort Chanel. She ran to look in the mirror and started crying. In her frail quivering voice she told me: "When I look in the mirror, it reminds me of that dumb dog. I don't like it Mommy." She was pale and continued to shake; her temperature was within normal range but she looked gaunt. This had been an exhausting day for both of us but especially for Chanel. She was stumbling over her words and was having a hard time discussing what happened as the officer continued to ask her questions. We both agreed we needed sleep. Chanel asked me to stay right by her side. We cuddled up together and attempted to sleep, but it didn't come easy.

The next morning as I reflected back on what Mrs. Dee told me last night at the hospital, about her dog being up-to-date with all his shots. I was somewhat relieved, but I wasn't sure I was getting all the information I needed. The first thing I did this morning was to call the veterinary clinic on Medford Avenue to report what had happened and to confirm the dog was up-to-date with all his shots. As the veterinarian technician at the clinic pulled up the dog's name on the computer, I heard a gasp over the phone. The technician proceeded to tell me that there was a note in the dog's file that read in bold letters "FEAR BITER." This dog was well known to this clinic, and the owners had been instructed several times to never bring the dog into the clinic prior to heavily sedating and muzzling him first!!

As time went on Chanel continued to complain of pain at the site of the dog bite. She was very self-conscious of the scar on her face and refused to have any school pictures taken of her. Thankfully she continued to love dogs, just not pit bulls. I explained to her that she must be cautious with all dogs, not just pit bulls. Sometimes out of the clear blue Chanel would start talking about the incident. "My teacher tried to pull the dog off of me, but when she did, the dog still had a big piece of my lip and face in his mouth. I kept begging her to call you but she wouldn't, she wouldn't even let me call 911. I couldn't believe the bad word she said, Mommy, the F-word"

Below is Chanel's own description of the dog attack, which she has asked to be included in this book.

It is July 5 2001

I am happy because I am going to my teachers aide house when I get home from summer school. I am waiting in the kitchen watching the clock my teachers aid should be here any min. a car puts up its my teacher I kiss my goodbye mom said to check in with her every hour I say yes mommy I will. We get to my teachers house her dog is locked up in a bedroom she tell me not to open the door I said ok I wont. I check in with mom every hour like she told me too. It is now 6:00 p.m. i call mom and ask her if it ok if I stay from dinner. I can tell that she didn't really want to but I beg her and she told me that she wants me home at 7P.m. not a min later. I hang up the phone I sit down at the kitchen table and I start to eat as I was eating one of her boys lets the dog out of the room my teacher tried to catch the dog by she couldn't so she just leaves the dog loose I go to get a together plate of food I went to pet the dog (just pet the dog) and the dog jumps up and bites me on the lip as the teacher aid trys to get the dog off me she is rips my lip with it. .when we get the dog to let go of my lip I remember slipping in the pool of blood I am dize and confused but one thought come to my mind I have to call my mom or 911 as I go to the phone my teacher aid takes the phone out of my hand SHE SAID NO GETIN THE F***ING CAR I AM TAKING YOU HOME . the pain was so bad but when my teachers aid said that I stared at her I have never heard anyone say that word but I knew that it was a bad word. I don't really remember to about the drive back home all I remember thinking was mom is go-ing to be so mad at me. As we pull up to the house I am crying the pain is back it hurts so bad. As my teachers aid knocks on the door and my mom opens the door my mom says oh my god what happen!!! My teacher tell my mom to calm down my mom told me to take the towel away from my lip there is a big hole where my lip should have been. My mom rushes me to the hospital. The first hospital was full they told us that we had to wait. Then we leave we go to the next hospital it was full mom told me to show them my face soo I did they take me right away. I am tired., cold I want the pain to stop. My mom is talking to my teacher asking her is your dog up to date with its shorts she told my yes. She asked my teacher why didn't you call 911 my teacher said why when she was little she was at a friends home and she got hurt and they wouldn't take her with out her mom there. It was getting late and I so tired mom was holding me. Finefully they took me. They told me to hold still I was stared and I didn't know what was going on they put a niel in my lip I yelled it hurt so bad. I thaink I fell asleep I don't remember much about getting fixed up. I do recalled the doctor asking me do I want me to num the other part of your lip? I said NO just do it didn't hurt I didn't feel it. My teachers aid in the room the hole time. I know that mom asked her questions but I don't know what the questions were. After I got fixed up went home I think it was 11:00 my dad was waiting for us. My mom told me to go sleep on the couch I was very tired. The next day mom called there vet to maked sure that the dog was up to date with all its shorts. The first that popped up on the screen was FEAR BITER.

Because the dog was a fear biter it had to come to vet mused and asleep. So my teacher new that her dog was a biter. The dog bit her son on the foot and the husband on the hand. Why would you keep a dog that like I never understand why.

Chanel also wrote a note to her birth mother Christine, to tell her about the incident.

Hi christine

I got bite by my teach dog. He was mean and made a hole in my face by mo mouth. It hurt real bad. But im no mad at dogs. So what r you do? I have another sis now. her name is rosina. so now I have 7. she had surgry on her hart but she is ok now. I would like to meet u but I don't knw where u are. My other sister has som pet rats, I think 4. They don't bite but I don like them. ok if u can writ to me back.

From Chanel

CHAPTER NINETEEN:

THE TORRES FAMILY MOVES TO FLORIDA

After struggling with Alonna's wheel chair on the heavy snow days during the winter, we finally put our Jayne Avenue home on the market on a Friday night in July 2001. The very next day, Saturday morning at 9:00 a.m., our home was under contract to neighbors down the street. They were renters with three young children. There was only one problem: We were not ready to move to Florida just yet because little Rosina was due to have her second open heart surgery. We had no clue our home would sell so fast. I was hoping for a sale in three to four months, not in eight hours! I wanted her to have the surgery in New York where the cardiologists knew her well. The new homeowners wanted to close as soon as possible. We put off closing for as long as we could, but we ended up agreeing to do a house swap with the buyers of our home and with the permission of their landlord. It would be sad to leave our home, but we knew that we had only sold the house not our wonderful memories.

The rental home didn't have air conditioning, and that was a big concern to me because little Rosina needed to stay cool. When I toured the home, it was in the evening so the heat was less noticeable. The lights were dim, and when the female renter took me on a tour,

Unfortunate house swap

for some reason she blocked the kitchen entrance in such a way that I didn't realize she was preventing me from going in there. I peeked over her shoulder and it seemed like everything was in order, the countertops were clear. I wasn't paying close attention. After all, we were only going to be there for four to six weeks.

On July 30, 2001, at 11:00 a.m. we gave the keys to the new owners. My hands trembled as I handed them over to the male home buyer. After all this was our beautiful home for many years, and I loved everything it represented. It was a sad day for all of us, but I trusted that time would soften our sadness and we would be able to savor all the wonderful memories.

The house swap was a disaster. The Long Island heat and humidity was unbearable. Our rented U-Haul truck was so small we had to make many trips back and forth. As we were unloading the contents of the truck into the small space of our temporary rental, we saw up close and in daylight all the filth and I mean filth! The shower had dirty dark water stains dripping down the wall, and clumps of dark hair and white mush rolled up by the drain. There was a strong urine smell around the toilet, not to mention in the basement where we found and counted three hundred beer bottles, urination on the concrete and dirt floor and mice! Old toothpaste was caked on the back wall of the sink. The oven was disgusting, as was the refrigerator, which had a pool of hardened red liquid at the bottom. I sat down and cried. I didn't want my girls living like this, not even for six weeks!

One of the wretched appliances.

There was absolutely no time to find another rental place for that short period of time for our family of five. After loading and unloading the truck about 20-25 times we had finally piled all the boxes in the living room. We were only going to unpack what we absolutely needed.

After a long and tearful end to a stressful day, Armando and I put clean sheets on the beds. We were all so exhausted from the move. One by one the little ones came to comfort me, kissing me and telling me, "It will be okay Mommy, don't worry."

Armando fell asleep almost immediately and so did Rosina, but Alonna, Chanel and I just could not fall asleep. We were kept awake by all the strange noises; from the house settling to dogs barking outside and cars passing by, even at 2:00 a.m. At one point I looked over at Alonna and then Chanel to see that they had finally fallen asleep. My eyelids were getting heavy and though I was fighting to keep them open, for a second or two I lost the battle. With my eyes finally shut tight, I found myself slapping a few flies away. Then I felt things crawling on me. I tried my best not to frighten the girls but I couldn't help myself. I started screaming. The place was full of roaches! Oh my God, what had we gotten ourselves into? Everyone was awake now, the girls were crying, and Armando was trying to calm us all down as he chased the bugs away. I knew those ugly crawling creatures would return as soon as the lights went off, so we slept with the lights on throughout the night.

I refused to use the bathroom, even after scrubbing it with bleach five times. Each time I needed to use the bathroom or have a shower I ran back just a few houses down Jayne Avenue to Gail's house, being careful not to look next door at house number 63, as it was just too painful. Sometimes we drove 20 minutes to my daughter Alexa's place to take our showers.

Our rental apartment in Florida wouldn't be ready until October 10th so we didn't have much of a choice but to wait the few weeks. Many of my Jayne Avenue neighbors offered to come clean the rental house for me, but I turned them down. I had already tried cleaning out the bathroom, but still couldn't bring myself to use it. We didn't use the kitchen either, eating every meal out. The landlord came to spray for the roaches. We had to make the best of the few weeks we had there.

As luck would have it, Rosina's surgery was put off for six months. There was no way I would be staying in the rental house that long, so it was easy to make the decision that Rosina's second open heart surgery would be done in Florida. I called my daughter, Trudy, in Florida to look into whether we could expedite the move-in date, or find another place that would meet our needs. Fortunately, there was an apartment available on September 23, 2001. We were all getting psyched, and couldn't wait for the big day.

My neighbors, Gail and Julie, each gave us a going away party. Julie was a great cook and invited us over for a wonderful sit down dinner on two separate occasions; she also invited Gail and Dale. Gail had a wonderful back-yard BBQ party and opened her home for us while we were in distress. These were true friends who I would miss dearly! I am forever grateful for the wonderful memories they contributed to the lives of my family, far overpowering the bad memories in that rental home. Many other neighbors helped with packing, loading and home cooked dinners. There was no other neighborhood in America like this one.

Chanel's behavior had been pretty good through all this craziness and she did her best to deal with the awful mess we had gotten ourselves into.

About 8:55 a.m. on 9/11/2001, my daughter, Alexa, pulled her car up to our rental home and blurted out "Mom, did you hear? A plane just crashed into one of the twin towers!"

I stood at the curb next to her car in disbelief. Five minutes later we heard the announcement on the car radio that a second plane had hit the World Trade Center. Armando and I scrambled to find out about friends and family that lived or worked in Manhattan. One of my friends lost her brother in one of the twin towers. Our family members were okay, but frightened. Armando's nieces had to walk for miles to get from Manhattan to Brooklyn. All public transportation had been suspended. Armando and I did our best not to alarm the girls by reading the paper and watching all the horrific news clips on one of our neighbor's televisions.

On September 24, 2001, Alexa, and her friend helped load up a very large U-Haul truck and headed to Florida with all our worldly possessions. The truck was so full that, whenever we opened up the back door, something fell out. There wasn't even room for a hairpin. The next day, Armando and I got into the front seat of our van while the girls piled into the back seat giggling with each other and excited to get on with their new lives in Florida. We had just one small suitcase each. It was both a sad and happy day for all of us.

After saying our good-bye's to our wonderful Jayne Avenue neighbors who had been in our lives for well over 25 years, we left Long Island. I will always keep Long Island in my heart. It is where I was born and raised. It is where the Morgan family was well known as the owners of the Bellport Casino.

Two days later, on September 27, 2001, (on my birthday) after an arduous drive, we arrived at the corner of Gandy and 4th Street North where Apt. 10234 would become our next temporary home in St. Petersburg, Florida. Our daughters, Trudy, Alexa, Jessica; and Alexa's friend, had already unloaded the truck for us and put a birthday cake in the refrigerator for me along with a much appreciated bottle of wine. This was a wonderful birthday gift from my daughters. While it had taken Armando and me more than four days to load the moving truck, it had taken only one day for my daughters and a friend to unload it into this small apartment and put everything neatly away.

As I walked into this nice clean apartment I just wanted to collapse with joy. "Gosh, I love my daughters."

We took a quick tour through the small, standard apartment; three bedrooms, two bathrooms, small kitchen, living room and a cozy eating area right next to the kitchen. Alonna and Chanel would share a room, Rosina would sleep in our room, and the third bedroom was perfect for storage. The walls were white and boring, and the wall-to-wall carpet was the usual apartment beige. I loved the screened-in lanai, and pictured myself having a cup of warm cocoa out there early in the morning, gazing out at the picturesque, serene and peaceful wooded nature preserve area that I'm sure housed lots of Florida snakes, turtles and other creatures. The air smelled flowery and was thick with humidity that flattened my hairstyle. Just outside the master bedroom was a sandy play area with swings and a few slides perfect for the girls. At that point all five of us were beyond tired from the long trip. Thanks to my wonderful daughters, the beds were already set up, but despite our exhaustion we found it hard to sleep in this strange new place.

Alexa unhitched her car from the back of the moving van, preparing to head back to New York. Saying good-bye to Alexa was the hardest part. As I watched her walk away from the apartment, my heart felt like it was breaking in two. I will never forget that moment! I wanted to live near all my children and didn't like the fact that three of my daughters would remain in New York, about 1,200 miles away. Alexa and Dana had already informed me that, they would NEVER move to Florida. (Though that's what we had said, also, and now there we were!)

In the morning, I was greeted by a swift tropical flowery breeze as I opened the back door from the kitchen, I loved the view. What I didn't like were the large black snakes that slithered across the lawn from the nature preserve onto the sidewalk just outside our apartment. "They're just sunbathing," a neighbor said, "If you're going to live in Florida, get used to this, it's part of Florida living and the black snakes are harmless." "I'm not sure I can get used to this," I replied. The girls also found some really strange bugs, not like any we have ever seen in New York. Chanel was most amazed with the ubiquitous speedy little lizards; it was hard to walk without stepping on one she would cry out.

By the end of the week we learned our way around town and met several more neighbors. I was already starting to have concerns about some of the odd ones, especially since Chanel had already made friends with some peculiar men.

After registering the girls for school, I found out the bus would not provide door-to-door pick up service as we had been granted in New York due to the girl's special needs; mostly because the large bus would have difficulty maneuvering around the apartment complex parking lot. The girls were both assigned a bus stop right on very busy 4th Street, just outside the complex. Each morning Armando or I walked the girls to the bus stop, waiting with them until they were on the bus. Two homeless men in wheel chairs begged for money on the corner of 4th and Gandy. Chanel had already asked if she could go talk to the man in the wheel chair and I'm sure if we hadn't been there she would have already approached them.

"This is not a safe bus stop for my girls," I complained to the transportation department.

I wasn't sure how long Armando and I would be able to maintain our promise to each other of waiting one full year before buying a home in St. Petersburg. We wanted to make sure this was where we wanted to settle down for the next ten years or so. The area seemed to be meeting all of our needs, except for some of the strange people we have met.

We especially loved All Children's Hospital, which was about six to seven miles away and staffed every imaginable pediatric specialist.

Alonna and Chanel started at Tyrone Middle School on October 25, 2001, shortly after getting settled in our new apartment. The school was right in St. Petersburg, only a few miles away. Their first day went well. Chanel met Officer Carven, also known as Officer OC and they quickly developed a great relationship. He took Chanel under his wing and always did his best to keep her from going down the wrong path. On one occasion, Chanel came home with a music CD. When I asked her where she got it, she told me her friend gave it to her, but she couldn't produce the name of the friend. I immediately called Officer OC and told him I thought Chanel may have taken the CD. Could he help me out? We set up an appointment with Chanel's teacher,

Chanel, Officer OC and me. One by one we arrived in an office with a long intimidating table surrounded by high back chairs. Chanel was crying so hard her lips were turning blue. She was so upset to have disappointed Officer OC. He told her about the local juvenile detention center, saying "You don't want to end up there, Chanel." Of course we couldn't have known at this point that she would indeed end up at the Pinellas County Juvenile Detention Center and several other detention centers later on down the road, or what she would be doing there. But we'll get to that later in the story. Our intervention was effective. Chanel was embarrassed, and that was exactly the reaction I had hoped for.

Often at night I'd hear Chanel cry out in her nightmares, "NO, NO, STOP! STOOOO~~~P! "Someone get the dog off me!" When I attempt to comfort her she would yell, "The dog followed me to Florida and he's outside my window, Mommy!" None of my words comforted her. Each night, she told me, "I know you don't believe me, Mommy, but the dog *IS* outside. He came to get me, Mommy, he's going to attack me again!"

On November 13, 2001, we had an 8:00 a.m. appointment with Dr. Lundy, the behavior specialist at All Children's Hospital. After talking to him on the phone about Chanel's nightmares we were able to secure several appointments. These appointments continued twice a week for well over a year. On our last visit, Dr. Lundy called me in the room by myself and gave me his final report. "I have diagnosed Chanel with post-traumatic stress disorder." He told me that in all the years he had counseled children, he had never experienced anything like this, even with those children who had witnessed horrific abuse. He said when he asked those children "what was the worst thing that ever happened to you," some would respond with the following: "Well, I fell off my bike and got hurt," or, "I lost my favorite doll." They would say nothing about the horror they had witnessed. When he asked Chanel the very same question, she answered without hesitation: "The dog attack." She even drew a graphic picture of that day; blood splattered all over the floor, a large hole on the left side of her face and a large laceration mid-center below her bottom lip. Mrs. Dee was standing behind her with the dog as blood was dripping from his mouth. Dr. Lundy gave me a copy of this picture for my records. Chanel's nightmares continued for many years, although they diminished with time. She continued to love animals and still wanted to become a veterinarian someday.

While the girls were at school, Armando and I spent time riding around looking for a quiet little neighborhood for the girls, paying little attention to our promise of waiting for one year before buying a home. One day we found the perfect home in a quiet neighborhood without a swimming pool. The house had a large living room, a den, a formal dining room, a big kitchen, a second dining area just beyond the den, large sliding glass doors leading out to the lanai, a laundry room and a two-car garage. Beyond the lanai was a very large backyard. I absolutely loved the layout of this three-way split four-bedroom home. Alonna would have the larger guest bedroom with her own bathroom.

We signed the contract and had only three weeks to wait until our move-in date. Unlike our sad experience of leaving our home in Patchogue, we were looking forward to this move. I wondered if the present owners were feeling the pain of leaving this beautiful home where they had raised their two sons, in fact, they had the home custom-built.

The Torres family moved into our new home on January 3, 2002. Spontaneous joyful laughter filled the house as the girls ran around yelling, "Yeah! This is our house!! Yeah!" Armando and I relished the thought of creating a lifetime of memories for the girls in this house. Each child ran to her pre-chosen room and started planning how she wanted her room set up and decorated. The move took us about three days to complete. Soon after moving in, we quickly made Alonna's bedroom and bathroom wheelchair accessible.

On March 8, 2002, I started my first job in Florida, at a healthcare facility as the nursing supervisor, less than one mile away from our home. My co-worker, Alexa M. and I worked well together covering each other's shifts when needed. After less than three years at the smaller building, I was moved to the larger 272-bed facility. I continued with the same job capacity and same shift. I continue to work there to this day.

A few months later in June 2002, Chanel got her first job just two houses away. She was hired to take care of our neighbor's eight parrots, on a regular basis, training them, keeping them clean, giving them fresh food and, socializing them by playing games with them. Chanel was still over-confident, something I worried about when it came to the beak power of larger parrots. After visiting and talking to the neighbor I was assured that

Chanel would not be allowed to handle all the birds, only a chosen few that were very friendly. Her dedication to the birds was beyond belief, so much so that she never wanted to call off sick, even when her knee was hurting or she had an upset stomach. She'd watch the clock 45 minutes before the start of work, asking every five minutes, "Mom is it time for me to leave yet?" Chanel quickly demonstrated the kind of work ethic that every employer longed for.

On October 16, 2002, Armando and I were ready to open up our large new home to children who needed us. We began classes for medical foster care here in Florida. After we completed the classes we received our "Medical Foster Care License" and would work with "Help A Child," an agency that helped babies with special needs. The medical foster care program allowed a foster baby with a chronic medical condition to grow and develop in a licensed family setting. They arrived, one after another, for the next several years, with their long lists of medical diagnoses and special needs. Some were on oxygen or required tube feedings, apnea monitors and many other supportive devices. We were doing what we loved once again, fostering children.

On December 14, 2002, the Torres family began a nine-day trip to New York. We traveled by van since I refused to fly, after all, it was much more fun to drive. We sang loud silly songs all the way to New York, something you couldn't do on a flight full of grumpy passengers. My ears and attention could be one hundred percent on the girls. I was now their captive audience!

As we arrived on Jayne Avenue I could hear the girls in the

back seat: "Oh wow, look, there's Debbie's house," Look, they changed the color! Oh no, I don't like that, "Oh Mom, look what they did to that house!" "Mom, I miss it here" it seemed as though ten years had passed. We yelled out the names of who lived in each house. "There's Miriam and Roy's house, oh and look, that's where Mr. and Mrs. Tortarella lived, look look! That's Cathy's, and over there is Ruth's and across the street is where Kathy L. and her husband lived. As we got closer to house number 63, I could feel goose bumps popping up and down my arm like popped corn, as I choked back a few tears.

Rosina and our good friend and Jayne Avenue neighbor, Gail

Gail

"WOW, I want to move back!"

"Mom, Mom, they changed the color of our house" "It's their house now," I said, "and they can do what they want with their house just as we can do what we want with our new home in Florida." After visiting each one of our neighbors and driving through the town of Patchogue as if we were tourists, we were ready for a long nap at Alexa's home. Of course, we stopped to say hello to daughters Dana and Brendalyn and several other Patchogue buddies. We reminisced, each of us remembering something the other had forgotten. As our visit was about to come to an end, we shed a few tears, hugged our neighbors and said good-bye, with a promise to return soon.

We traveled back to Florida just in time to set up the most glorious Victorian Christmas tree for our second Christmas in Florida and our first Christmas in our new home. Yet for some reason the Christmas spirit escaped me.

My older daughters were scattered around New York and Florida in their own new homes, and I was missing New York more than ever! Three daughters remained in New York, with Trudy and Jessica a 45-minute drive from our new home in St Petersburg. The nest was emptying little by little and I hated it! I did my best to put on a good front for the children.

Due to her uncoordinated, awkward and impulsive moves, Chanel continued to break things and Armando and I started a yearly tradition of calculating all the damage she had done. This year we added five dishes, four glasses, a few bowls, the front light switch, the back lanai screen door latch, shelving, the venetian blinds in her room, and the two large front window cranks. We were unable to replace the cranks because that model was no longer available so we had to replace the windows at a costly price. Then there were several Christmas tree ornaments, the zipper on my purse, the recliner control, one lamp, a VCR that she jammed a DVD into and attempted to fix but that only made things worse. The DVD player was rendered un-repairable. The list continued. Chanel is swift and often unable to perform simple physical tasks smoothly and efficiently. I reminded her often that when she meets with resistance she should stop and call an adult to complete the task, but without a reminder at the exact moment, she doesn't stop, she just plows through. Often she wouldn't tell me that she had broken something. Then later on in the day or even days after when I happened to notice a broken switch or whatever was broken, she denied breaking it. "I swear, really, I didn't do it, I didn't, really, please believe me!" If one of the other kids came forward to tell us they saw her do it, she sometimes would admit it, and other times she adamantly continued to deny it.

On March 7, 2003, Rosina had surgery for her cleft palate. That surgery took a toll on all of us. She did not do well and remained in the hospital in the ICU for an extended period of time. Armando and I took turns being at her side while the other one stayed home with a watchful eye on Chanel. Rosina was refusing to eat or drink and became seriously dehydrated requiring IV fluids and close monitoring due to her cardiac status. While we were here, she had a full cardiac workup and it was determined that she didn't need her second open heart surgery for a few more years. Magically her cardiac status had stabilized for now anyway.

On April 9, 2003, I picked Chanel up from school because she was having difficulty walking. I took her to the emergency room at All Children's Hospital. After a few hours in the ER and a knee brace for her dislocated knee, we headed home with the hopes of a few hours to nap before I went off to work that night. I often went work after nights like this and never said a word to my co-workers. Other times, I just blurted out all my daily woes (a temporary cathartic remedy).

Friday, June 20, 2003 was a very exciting day. A bird breeder friend of one of our neighbors came to visit us. Richard arrived with three red-sided Eclectus parrots (with an expensive price tag, I might add). Chanel played with all three of the birds and picked one out. He was a

14 week old, male parrot, and she called him, Mikey! Over time, Chanel trained Mikey to sleep in the bed with her for six consecutive hours, right on her pillow next to her head, without having an incontinent accident. She also trained him to talk, play dead, and throw a ball as well as many other tricks. When Chanel gave most of her attention to her pets, it kept her out of trouble. Although she was fantastic at keeping the cage clean and the parrot well fed, she did some damage while wheeling the large cage around. There were several gouges on the wall in her room, as well as the door to the lanai, where Chanel takes the cage to and from the yard for hosing off. She would often bring the cage back inside without wiping it down, causing water leakage on our hard-wood oak flooring. Urgh! We fixed one problem and created another.

On August 2, 2003, we attended our first Florida bird show, held at the St. Petersburg Coliseum. As we arrived to a very full parking lot, the kids were excited and couldn't wait to get inside to see the many different vendors and bird toys. The walls were lined with one bird cage after another, and then one huge aviary-like cage caught Chanel's eye. The cage cost more than $3,000. Chanel couldn't stop begging me to buy it, as though she was asking for a seventy-five cent pack of gum. As we walked around the show room, Chanel continued to beg me to buy all kinds of unnecessary toys and other parrot gadgets. She had so much for her parrot already.

"But Mom, he needs a new one. Please, PLEASE, can we buy this?" Like most kids her age, she had no clue how much three thousand dollars was. Armando and the other girls enjoyed the day, checking out the different bird breeds and vendors. What we thought would be a cheap family day turned out to be rather expensive. Although we didn't get the three thousand dollar aviary, we did spend way more than we intended.

I guess one parrot wasn't enough because on September 14, 2003 we bought Danny Boy. He was an eight-month-old African Grey Parrot from Animal House in Pinellas Park. We went in there to buy a $5 item for Mikey. Chanel now had several smaller birds and two larger parrots. She kept busy keeping them clean, happy and well fed. To prevent further damage to the doors or our oak flooring, I set new rules that only Armando or I were allowed to take the cages out through the back lanai doors.

On January 15, 2004, Chanel and Rosina started speech therapy in our home with Maria, who was a wonderful therapist. Maria came several times a week and was very dedicated. She truly enjoyed working with the girls. Rosina's speech was affected even after her surgery for cleft palate repair and Chanel continued to deal with stuttering. Often Chanel complained that students in her school were making fun of her, mostly because of her stuttering. The more they made fun of her the more she stuttered. My older daughters were wonderful at getting her to slow down when she talked, preventing most of the stuttering. Brendalyn had also given her some calming techniques that worked most of the time. When I first heard Maria ask Chanel to sing her sentences, my mouth fell open in disbelief. Maria was right Chanel didn't stutter when she sang whatever she had to say.

On March 1, 2004, another adult daughter moved to Florida. Yeah!! Armando took a flight back to New York to help her pack all her belongings into a U-Haul truck. They both took turns driving the truck down to Florida, where she moved into a condo along with her two cats. We purchased the condo with the hopes my mother would move into it, but that never did happen.

On August 7, 2004, the bird show was back in town. Chanel was intent on getting a few new toys for Danny and Mikey. Surprise! Surprise! We also came home with Pedro, a huge yellow and gold macaw!! What was I thinking? Now we had five birds. I reminded Chanel that only Armando or I could move the cages outside for hosing-down. Chanel's dedication to her birds was unbelievable! Not only was she taking care of her own birds, she continued to take care of the neighbor's parrots. Her pets occupied any free time she had, keeping her happy and out of trouble.

On August 12, 2004, hurricane Charley arrived in Florida with a vengeance. Our family and foster children had to evacuate to a local elementary school. Keeping an eye on our children (especially Chanel) in this strange place was a challenge. One of the organizers picked up on the fact that we had special needs children and placed us in a private room. After two hours, the room was no longer private; 30-40 people now filled the room, making this an even bigger challenge. Chanel roamed around wanting to talk to EVERYONE! Armando and I were exhausted but we didn't dare shut our eyes until Chanel was ready to settle down. She was still overly friendly with strangers. When I asked, "Who was that, do you know him?" She almost always said, "Yes, I know him, he's real nice." Throughout this whole ordeal Chanel was so worried about the pets we had to leave behind and mumbled about them quietly, over and over again. Our wonderful neighbors that didn't evacuate kept us posted of any damage to our home or neighborhood. We got the "all clear" to return home the next day. Our neighborhood had several downed trees scattered around but no major damage. And the pets were fine. Oh, the joys of Florida living!

On September 26, 2004, it was time for Hurricane Jeanne, the fourth one that season. The storm arrived as a bad rain and wind storm. While the evacuation site at the school had medical staff on hand if needed, we weren't sure we could handle another evacuation like with Charley. It sure did take a toll on the family. Luckily, we did not get the direct hit from Jeanne and didn't have to evacuate for this one. Phew!

On December 7, 2004, Armando's younger brother Saul died. Armando needed to be with his family and for his brother's wake in Puerto Rico. While he was gone, my days were filled with appointments, home therapy sessions, behavior monitoring and many other tasks. Parenting is already an exhausting endeavor, but parenting a child with fetal alcohol syndrome takes things to an unimaginable level of physical and mental fatigue. The time went by quickly until Armando returned on December 12th.

The damage tally for 2004 added up to approximately $2,000. I'd tell Chanel she would have to pay for the things she broke but that never happened. There were several more dishes, glasses, two sets of window shades, the console in our new car, the sliding glass door locks AGAIN, the bathroom faucet, two towel racks, another over-head fan dial, a radio, the temperature dial on the stove, Alonna's closet doors, the bathtub drain lock, Alonna's shower door and TV, the overhead fan in her room, several CD covers and several more items.

CHAPTER TWENTY:

MORE TROUBLE
FOR CHANEL

It was New Year's Day, 2005 and Chanel had been up most of the night studying for a test scheduled for the next morning. She looked tired; her eyes were deeply-set with dark circles. She hadn't put her books down in hours. Every few minutes she came out to tell me she was worried about the upcoming test."Mom, you don't understand, I have to get a good grade, I just have to."

I told Chanel. "Sometimes over-studying was worse than under-studying. Relax." She could get so obsessed with studying that I would worry about her. I offered to take her out for a bite to eat but she turned me down, saying, she couldn't stop studying, she wanted to get a good grade. She seemed lost and distant.

The next day, I had my own worries to contend with. You see, I'm a big chicken when it comes to the dentist, and I had a 10:00 a.m. appointment for a routine cleaning. To calm my nerves, I had taken a small dose of Valium, 2.5 milligrams, but by the time my name was called, all the Valium had worn off. As usual, I laid my purse on the side table and sat in the reclining chair. The dental hygienist chatted with me briefly before leaving the room to retrieve a few things. As I sat there with my head cocked back on the headrest I started thinking about Chanel and how hard she had studied through the night. I couldn't recall if she had eaten breakfast that morning. What I had noticed was that she was a bundle of nerves, mumbling and repeating things to herself as she rushed down the front walk-way, skipping steps in a hurry to get to the school bus. "Mrs. Torres," (pause) "Mrs. Torres" the hygienist was calling my name softly, not wanting to frighten me out of my day-dream. She continued to chat as she got started with the cleaning, her hands in my mouth and God-awful buzzing sounds filling the air. Water was splashing on my face and paper bib, making it difficult for me to answer any of her questions with no more than, "UH-huh." My body was tense; all my muscles were locked in a rigid position, anticipating pain at any given moment. Then my cell phone began ringing and of course I wasn't able to answer it. The dental hygienist asked if I would like to answer my cell, "It could be something important," she added. She reached over to the side table to get my phone and handed it to me,

"Hello, who is this?" I say as I answer the phone.

"This is Officer Troy, your daughter Chanel is having a seizure here at the school." I was so confused, "Wait, wait a minute, you must mean Alonna, Chanel doesn't have seizures." At this point I could hear the officer asking the teachers in the background, "What's this student's name again? The mom is telling me this must be Alonna because Chanel doesn't have seizures." I could hear several distant voices yelling out, "IT'S CHANEL, NOT ALONNA, having the seizure." I asked the officer to call an ambulance and get her to All Children's hospital," I will meet her there." I jumped out of the dentist's chair, grabbed my purse, yanked off my bib, and ran for my car, almost banging into an incoming client. As I got into the ER, I was ushered into a large trauma cubicle where doctors and nurses were surrounding Chanel. Her body was thrashing violently, her legs kicking and, arms flailing. Her face was contorted. An IV was in her arm and the doctors were attempting to keep it in place. One of the ER doctors called me over to the side and proceeded to tell me that, they couldn't figure this out. "We have given her high doses of Phenobarbital through her IV and she continues to seize." "We're not sure what's going on and we need to do further investigation. She will be admitted for observation and will need a CT scan and an MRI, as well as an MRA. We have already done labs and we're waiting for the results. We are hoping for some answers soon."

I was so perplexed and couldn't think clearly. I feared the worst-case scenario. The thrashing finally stopped and Chanel was admitted to All Children's hospital with left-sided weakness as well as some paralysis. One of the doctors told me this could be "Todd's paralysis."

"What the heck is Todd's paralysis?" I asked. Although I'm a nurse, I had never heard of it." An ER nurse explained to me that Todd's paralysis was a neurological condition experienced by those who have epilepsy where their seizures are followed by temporary paralysis. There isn't any treatment, other then rest until the paralysis disappears.

"But Chanel doesn't have epilepsy, and she's never had a seizure." I was so puzzled. Was this the beginning of more trauma in Chanel's life?

I followed the nurses as they wheeled the gurney in and out of the elevator and then into a room near the nurses' station for close monitoring. Later that day Chanel was taken down to the radiology department for an MRI and other testing. The MRI showed torturous blood vessels on the right side of her brain, and they asked if any other family members had similar issues." "I don't know, Chanel is adopted," I replied.

On the second day of her admission, my friend came to the hospital for a visit and to give me a break from standing right by Chanel's side. She had been seizing on and off through the night, but nothing as bad as the day before. I was so worried and filled with fear for Chanel and what would be in store for her future. Before I left for the cafeteria I pleaded with my friend, "Please, PLEASE, don't leave her alone, not even for a minute."

When I arrived back in the room, my friend asked me to step outside and proceeded to tell me, "Listen something is weird, I saw Chanel smirk while she was thrashing around, really she did."

"I was so upset by this and I couldn't believe what I was hearing. Was she really saying that Chanel was faking this? Oh my God, how could she say such a thing? "How does someone fake a seizure? That's impossible!" After my friend left, I didn't leave Chanel's side for even one minute. On the third day of her admission, I was looking at Chanel's weak, pale and gaunt body. She looked exhausted, her eyes were sunken and she appeared to have lost some weight. The neurologist came in and asked me to step into the hall. As we got farther away from Chanel's room, he preceded to talk to me, "Mrs. Torres, Chanel is having pseudo seizures."

"WHAT, OH MY GOD, WHAT ARE YOU TELLING ME" I gasped."

"Mrs. Torres, these are not true seizures. She has been getting high doses of Phenobarbital in her IV, there is no way she could still be seizing" I reflected back on what my friend told me about the smirk. Was this more of Chanel's attention-seeking behavior? I returned to Chanel's bedside, and continued to watch her every move, and I didn't say anything to her about my conversations with the neurologist or my friend. Later on that day I saw for myself that Chanel had a smirk on her face as she spoke to one of our neighbors on the phone. She then began to have what looked like a petit mal seizure. I was very familiar with seizures, not only am I a nurse, but Rosina had frequent violent seizures, and Alonna also had them regularly before she thankfully outgrew them.

On January 7, 2005, Chanel was discharged from All Children's Hospital after much testing had been done. Our discharge papers instructed us to follow up with Dr. Mullen, a pediatric neurologist. The next few days just absolutely exhausted me. In my head I pictured myself as a cartoon-like caricature with a vacuum hose in my mouth that was sucking the life out of me! I was so tired and didn't know how I would be able to function at work. I just wanted to pass out on my bed. Chanel continued to have seizures, one after the other. During one of the seizures she fell hard onto the hardwood oak floor in her room, and I found myself wondering again, "Could she really be faking this? She is seriously hurting herself!" When researching pseudo seizures, I learned that it was recommended to completely ignore the seizures. It reminded me of advice I'd once heard about temper tantrums and mentioned in an earlier chapter: Tantrums are like a Broadway show, if there isn't an audience the show won't go on. Ignoring Chanel's seizures had to be one of the most difficult tasks I have EVER had to do! I even scolded her a few times in a harsh tone: "Chanel, cut it out NOW! I'm tired and just don't want to deal with this any longer!" Despite my disregard of her thrashing and hitting her head, arms, legs and just about every part of her body on the hard wood flooring and sometimes on nearby furniture, the seizures continued. After three days of my ignoring this behavior, the seizures started to diminish each day until they came to a complete halt. I wanted so badly to hug Chanel and talk to her. Something serious must have been going on in her head. She needed me and I felt like I couldn't be there for her. The first time that she went 24 hours without a seizure I treated her to a small shopping spree and commended her for controlling her seizures. She is adamant, saying: "I have no control over the seizures Mom, I'm not doing it on purpose, I swear!" I decided the best way to handle this was to not talk about the negative behavior and just admire, commend, and praise the good behavior.

At 8:30 a.m., on February 17, 2005, Chanel and I met with Dr. Mullen, bringing the MRI and MRA results as well as all her lab results. Dr. Mullen confirmed that these could be pseudo-seizures. He added that the tortuous blood vessels in her brain did need follow up, but that these were not the cause of pseudo seizures or any seizures.

I confronted Chanel and told her what the doctors were telling me. She began to cry uncontrollably, telling me, "I'm not faking, please believe me, Mom!"

I asked her, "What happened the day of your first seizure at school? "

"I was getting ready for a very hard test," she said, "I studied the whole night before and didn't get much sleep." I remembered how stressed she had been the night before. She wanted to get a good grade and studied most of the night. I did read that pseudo-seizures can be brought on by stress. After several weeks of diminishing seizure-like activity until it became non-existent, the Torres family resumed all regular activity, but still being very careful not to stress Chanel out!

Over the next few weeks Armando and I occupied Chanel with all the things she loved to do, first and foremost her animals. She absolutely loved animals especially dogs and parrots.

In March of 2005, we arranged for Chanel to bring her talking parrots to my job. She put on a show for my patients and they loved it. Chanel beamed with delight as each of the patients oooo'd and awwww'd at the many tricks Chanel's parrots performed.

Things seemed to be going smoothly. We talked to her teachers at school and asked them to please be careful not to give Chanel too much homework or school activity for fear the pseudo seizures would return. Her teachers were a great support and were very careful not to over load her with schoolwork. Chanel wasn't happy about this. She wanted to do the work just like her classmates. Chanel was somewhat of a perfectionist at times and wanted to get good grades even to the point of stressing herself out to the max and possibly triggering a pseudo seizure.

By May 23, 2005, the Torres family was in much need of a vacation. The last few months had taken us to a new level of urgency. Even when Armando and I had a good eight or nine hours of sleep or a three-day weekend off from work, our emotional and physical exhaustion never let up.

The weight of parenting a child with fetal alcohol syndrome can be daunting, to say the least. So from May 23-27, 2005, Armando and I took our family and our foster children on a trip to Disney World for fun and relaxation. Thankfully, it was an uneventful trip. We all desperately needed this break from our everyday hectic life.

Just as all the drama and trauma from Chanel's seizure episodes were ending, on June 24, 2005, Chanel was hit by a car while riding her bike only two houses down from ours. I was vacuuming the living room floor when I heard a loud knock at the door. Alonna and Rosina were in their rooms and Chanel was outside riding her bike, or so I thought. When I answered the door, the neighbor's son was attempting to tell me something, but he was stumbling over his words. "Chaaa-Chaa-Chaaanel was hit by a car!" he finally blurted out. As I looked across the street I saw a crowd of people looking down at something on the ground. I ran to the crowd, plunging right to the middle only to find Chanel lying down on the neighbor's lawn. Several people had witnessed the accident and told me that "her body was caught on the underside of the car and dragged for a short distance." When the car had finally come to a full stop, Chanel had gotten up and walked, very unsteadily, to the neighbor's lawn, where she had collapsed and had now begun to seize. Her mangled bike lay next to her.

I attempted to comfort Chanel as she was seizing. Someone had already called the paramedics, and they arrived seconds after I did. Back again to the ER, it wasn't long ago we were there with Chanel for her seizures! After many X-rays to check her arm, hand and wrist for fractures, none were found. Chanel was diagnosed with a concussion, and bad road burn to her back. The nurses were just as amazed 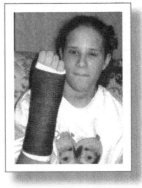 as I was that there were no fractures. A nurse removed all the debris; pebbles, grass and dirt that had embedded into the badly excoriated area covering a large portion of her back. I reflected back on what I once read about victims diagnosed with fetal alcohol syndrome; some don't make it to adulthood due to trauma or accidental death. Will this be Chanel's fate? This was her second near-death experience, the first being the attack by the pit bull a few years back. My sense of responsibility was reaching new heights. As it was, I already never wanted to leave her alone for a second.

The accident was no fault of hers, many witnesses said. She was riding her bike on the side of the road when a young man driving above our neighborhood speed limit hit her from behind.

On June 28, 2005, Chanel visited Dr. Chimino for a follow-up appointment after the car accident and ER visit. Though the X-rays from the ER were negative for fracture, Chanel was complaining of pain in her right hand. Dr. Chimino ordered further X-rays and once again the results were negative.

On July 15, 2005, Chanel saw Dr. Chimino for a second time as she continued to complain of pain. A third set of X-rays were taken and the results once again were negative. He referred us to the orthopedic department at All Children's Hospital. We quickly scheduled an appointment and a fourth set of X-rays were taken. "There, there's the fracture, right on the scaphoid bone in her right wrist," the orthopedist pointed out. He continued to tell us that sometimes even with treatment, fractures of the scaphoid bone can take a long time to heal, due to the poor blood supply of that particular bone. Unfortunately this proved to be the case for Chanel. We joked about the bright purple cast she would have to wear for the next few weeks. Since Chanel was unable to use her right hand, she was allowed to utilize a special typewriter in class. To date Chanel continues to experience pain in her right hand, especially when she forgets to use her left hand giving her right hand (her dominant hand) a rest. Her mangled bike remained in the garage and we never replaced it.

Chanel wrote a letter to her birth mother Christine, telling her about the accident (we had no way of getting this letter or any of her other letters to Christine, so we put all the letters Chanel would write in a box with the hope of someday handing them to her):

Hi Christine,

I love to ride my bike I would ride my bike all day up and down our street. I would go in peoples drive ways. Mom would tell me not to do that. I don't know why I wasn't listening to what she was telling me to do I like to ride my bike very fasted. I don't like to wear my hult.

Was coming out of my narbles drive way and on my way home I was on the side of the road when I got hit my car while I was riding my bike. I was dragged under the car. I don't remember much but I remember that my wrist hard really bad. My mom said that I collapsed on the side of the road. I went to the hospital my back was stretched up. The doctors took a x-ray of my arm they said it wasn't broken. I went home with a silt on my arm. I took a rest for 3 days. After 3 days my arm felt like it was fire. So we went to get a nothing x ray again they doctors said it wasn't broken. I was using my hand it hurt really bad. 3 moths go by with me still in a lot of pain in my hand. We went to get another app they doctors took some more x rays. Right away they told me that my arm was broken. I was in a cast for 6 weeks. It was very hard to not to the things that I loved to do. In school my teachers let to type out my work because I couldn't write with a case on my arm. I still have pain in my arm and writing is very painful typing didn't hurt as much.

Chanel

On September 2, 2005, I confronted Chanel about some disturbing behavior we had been seeing for several months. Chanel would retreat to her room a few times a week and we would hear her arguing with someone-except there was no one in the room with her. On this day I decided I would walk into her room right in the middle of one of these arguing episodes. "Who are you talking to Chanel?"

"Who's in here with you," I asked Chanel, as I looked under her bed and in the closet.

"No one, Mom, there's no one in here, I'm talking to my birds…" she said.

On September 15, 2005, we had a visit with psychiatrist Dr. Darby, along with a female intern who worked closely with him. Chanel and I were escorted into the office and directed towards the stereotypical sofa on the far end of the room. I don't recall the intern's name. As Chanel and I sat side by side on the sofa, the intern asked Chanel many questions as to why she talked to herself. "I don't know," was Chanel's response. After speaking with the intern for about 25 minutes, Chanel was given a script for Seraquil 25 mg BID. "Oh, here we go again, another MAGIC PILL," I think to myself. I didn't know they made a pill that could stop someone from arguing with themselves.

On September 22, 2005, Matter Brothers Furniture delivered the new bedroom sets and bedding that we had ordered for each of the girls. Chanel's was a very expensive set that she picked out herself. It was a country white, four-poster bed, dressed in beautiful new sheets with a pink, yellow and blue multi-colored quilt with different patterns including large cabbage roses and calico prints. The bed was adorned with puffy, pink and lacy throw pillows that we had picked out together. Chanel was so excited she couldn't wait to go to bed that night.

Week after week I heard strange noises from Chanel's room at night. I had no idea what was causing the noises, but I chose to ignore it. When the noise continued for months, my curiosity grew out of control. One night as I was hearing the rickety noises I opened her door abruptly to find her jumping on her new expensive bed with full force, just as if it were a trampoline. Here she was at the age of fourteen and a half, jumping like a three year old! I told her she must stop doing this, or she would lose her television privileges for three days. She didn't stop. Next I threatened her outdoor privileges, then her telephone usage, but she just wouldn't stop. Her new mattress had a large hollowing depression in the center from her repetitive jumping and bouncing.

Sometime at the end of the month I went into Chanel's room while she was at school. I was impressed at how neat and clean her room was, but as I bent down to pick something up, one of the bed posts fell to the floor! I was in total shock and I just couldn't imagine how this could have happened. It wasn't a clean break; it looked like someone had worked hard at removing the post using physical force. I said nothing to Chanel when she came home from school, but I noticed that whenever I went near her door she ran to me and asked what I needed. "Oh nothing," I would reply. I teased her this way for a week or so, not letting on that I knew very well about the broken bedpost. Whenever I would tell her I was going to clean her room, ta-dah! Magically her room became spotless without my assistance or encouragement. On the big reveal day, I walked into Chanel's bedroom, where she was lying down on her bed. I stood very close to the broken bedpost, which you'd never know was broken unless you touched it and it fell to the floor. I asked her to help me turn her mattress over, explaining that this should be done every few months or so, especially with a newer bed. As I expected, she did everything she could to convince me it didn't need to be done today. Finally I ended the charade "Sit down, Chanel, I know about the post, and I want an answer NOW. How did this happen?" As Chanel continued to deny breaking the post or even knowing that the post was broken, I took away one privilege after another until she had lost four privileges and finally gave in and admitted to what she had done. She had broken the post off by swinging from it over and over with all her might until it snapped. Why did she do it? The post was in her way while she watched television! Can you believe it? To date Chanel is the only child in our home without a television in her room.

On September 23, 2005, our follow-up appointment at 10:45 a.m. with psychiatrist Dr. Darby and his intern was unproductive. I waited for her to direct Chanel into a recumbent position on the sofa, just like in the Hollywood movies. Next, Sigmund Freud would jump out from behind the door and begin to hypnotize Chanel. Of course none of that happened. If the sofa was there to relax us it certainly didn't. I did most of the talking, reporting that Chanel had continued to talk to herself, usually at night and only when she was in her room alone. She was gaining weight from the Seraquil and complained of feeling dizzy most of the day. The intern assured me, "It takes time to work, give it a few more months." We were given a refill prescription for Seraquil and off we went.

On October 11, 2005, an early morning phone call from Armando's family brought some sad news, Armando's brother William Torres had died at 4:00 p.m. in Brooklyn, New York. Brendalyn and Armando flew out to attend the wake and to support the family. They returned to Florida a few days later. I was on high behavior alert when Armando was away, doing the work of two.

For Chanel's 16th birthday on December 31, 2005 she was given the choice of a computer or a birthday party, and she chose the computer. This turned out to be the best choice for two reasons. Chanel had become pretty computer savvy and often helped family and friends with computer woes. And the surprise benefit was that the computer became a very effective punishment tool.

When she did something that she shouldn't have, I held her computer as ransom for a few days and restricted her other privileges. Of course this was a last resort. We did our best to be good role models. We also reminded Chanel on a regular basis what was expected of her as well as what the consequences would be if she continued with the undesirable behavior. Chanel absolutely hated when her computer was taken away, and often tried to bargain with me.

"Can't you take my CD player or something else instead of the computer?"

"No, I will take your computer; I get faster results this way, and taking away what you want me to take away just defeats the purpose."

Sometimes it worked, sometimes it didn't, but she was often very apologetic and seemed to be sincere with her apologies, at least for the moment.

On January 5, 2006, Chanel saw her pediatrician Dr. Cimino for a morning appointment. He always knew how to talk to her and guide her and she was comfortable talking to him. He reminded me of the Norman Rockwell paintings. On this day, Chanel was hoping for advice on controlling some of her behaviors. She continued to be defiant, doing things she knew she was not allowed to do. She simply refused to follow the house rules. This was not usually out of anger. She was almost always sweet and rarely disrespectful, which is better than I could say about some other teenagers! The previous week, I had been talking about Chanel's fetal alcohol syndrome and some of these undesirable behaviors to the receptionist at the pediatrician's office. Two women over heard me and interjected.

One said, "Well, my daughter does the same thing and she doesn't have fetal alcohol syndrome."

The other woman added, "That's all normal behavior for a six year old." I stunned them both when I told them Chanel was 16, not six. I wish I had a camera to capture the look on their faces.

Victims of fetal alcohol syndrome mature much slower than their peers and most never mature fully. It's like having a two year old for four years, a four year old for the next four years, and a six year old for the next few years. Then at some point their maturity comes to a complete halt never catching up to their chronological age even as an adult. On occasion, Chanel would go into a fit of giggling or find herself crying over something that wasn't very sad. Her emotional behaviors were disproportionate to what was actually occurring.

About a month earlier, Chanel had met a woman at a neighbor's house and they talked for about 45 minutes. At the end of the conversation the woman told Chanel she enjoyed her company and she hoped to see her next year when she came back to St Petersburg to visit her family. They hugged and parted. For the rest of the day, Chanel cried uncontrollably, saying, "I'm going to miss her so much, Mom, she is my friend, I don't know what to do, I wish she wouldn't leave!"

"Chanel, you just met this women today," I explained, trying to both comfort her and teach her, "It takes time to develop a friendship. You will meet many people that will come and go from your life. You can't become attached to every person you meet."

CHAPTER TWENTY-ONE:

MEETING TRENT

One evening in February 2006 shortly after dinner, Armando answered the phone in another room. I could hear him talking to someone but I didn't pay attention to what they were talking about. When he came back into the kitchen he said, "Oh that was Cathy from New York on the phone. She told me Rosina's mother had another baby, a little boy. He's about three months old but he still hasn't left the hospital." Here we go again! The very next morning I called the Suffolk County Department of Social Services in New York to inquire about this little boy. I didn't receive a return call for a few days.

"Hello Mrs. Torres, this is Mrs. G., I understand you were inquiring about a baby boy that is in our custody. What can I do for you?" I questioned her about his adoption status and informed her that I had already adopted his sister Rosina formally known as Reanna.

"Mrs. Torres, this is a VERY sick little boy. We are not sure home placement is in the plan right now," She continued, "He needs several open heart surgeries."

I continued to call the agency for the next few months to express our desire to foster and possibly adopt the boy. We called numerous times with our questions finding it more and more difficult to speak to the correct person. We hadn't said a word to Rosina about her little brother at that point.

Chanel continued to see Dr. Lundy, the behavioral specialist, two days a week, for her post-traumatic stress disorder from the dog bite incident. He agreed to continue with her sessions for several more months. I told Dr. Lundy that we had plans for another Disney World vacation to help Chanel forget about that awful day. Of course he smiled and wished us well.

The pain in Chanel's right hand had been unbearable, so before we left for Disney World she had cortisone injections in her hand.

"This should relieve the agony for the next two to three days," Dr. Bard (the hand specialist) told us.

On March 18, 2006, we left early for our three-day vacation. Everyone was in very good spirits. The cortisone was effective, Chanel wasn't feeling any pain, and the trip to Disney World was a huge success. There were two brief moments of panic when I lost sight of Chanel, only to find out she was right nearby. I was tempted to put a leash around her waist.

On March 31, 2006, once again I placed a call to New York to inquire about Trent, Rosina's baby brother. "He's in a fragile state right now." the nurse told me, "He's scheduled to undergo emergency open heart surgery for fluid build-up around his heart tomorrow morning. "

I didn't even know this little boy and yet my heart ached for him. We continued to keep this quiet from Rosina, though I did tell Chanel and Alonna, and of course Armando. I didn't want to give Rosina false hopes if we were unable to adopt Trent. I hoped Chanel could keep this to herself; she usually had quite a hard time keeping a secret.

After the pain in Chanel's hand returned with a vengeance and had become unbearable, on April 3, 2006, she had her first appointment at a pain management clinic at St. Anthony's and we met with Dr. Len at 3:00 p.m. Since all other measures to control the pain had failed, he was recommending a procedure called ganglion nerve block, which involves an anesthetic injection given in the neck area. It was supposed to numb the nerves in her right arm and neck area temporarily. This will be done in three steps," he told us. We scheduled all three appointments, because Chanel was anxious to get this over with. She was having a challenging time using her non-dominant hand, sometimes forgetting and suffering relentless pain after using her right hand. The hand therapy sessions with the TENS machine (Transcutaneous electrical nerve stimulation) had been somewhat effective, but any pain relief was short-lived. We were really hoping this new procedure would get her back on track.

At the end of June, 2006, we signed Chanel up for yoga classes as a stress management tool. What would be normal everyday stressors for others were always magnified for Chanel. While stress is necessary for life and for survival, it becomes harmful when it becomes overwhelming. She really enjoyed the yoga lessons and made a lot of adult friends. She would come home and demonstrate the relaxing techniques she learned and put her yoga to good use whenever she felt the need.

After many phone calls to the Suffolk County Department of Social Services in New York, we finally heard from Rosina and Trent's birth mother Tammy on July 10, 2006. She told me her court hearing for abandonment charges related to Trent was happening that day in Hauppauge, New York. She also told me that she planned to request that Trent be adopted by the Torres family. We learned later that when Tammy showed up at court, her words were slurred and her walk was unsteady as she meandered up to the podium. As a result, the hearing was cancelled until further notice.

On July 26, 2006, Chanel had her first ganglion nerve block, but it was not successful in relieving her pain. Several doctors and friends had told us that the procedure is usually effective, yet the pain in her right hand continued and sometimes it was so unbearable Chanel would retreat to her room and cry. It was hard watching her suffer like that. We had hoped the next two nerve blocks would be effective; she was way too young to have this much pain. Chanel was not a complainer, nor was she whiny when she wasn't feeling well. So when she would tell me her pain was at ten out of ten, I knew it was pretty bad.

On August 2, 2006, Chanel had her second ganglion block at the pain management clinic at St. Anthony's. She also continued with her hand therapy waiting a few days after the ganglion block procedure, as required. Again, the procedure was not effective in reducing Chanel's pain. Some days she experienced more pain than other days. It all depended on how much she used her right hand as opposed to her non-dominant hand.

On August 9, 2006, Dr. Len performed the third and final ganglion block, this time at 11:00 a.m. At this point there had been zero relief from the constant pain in Chanel's right hand, and this third treatment made no difference.

In the early morning, of September 15, 2006, we spoke with Barbara, who was the same case worker we had been assigned to for Alonna and Chanel. Now we were talking about adopting Trent. This was such a convoluted case; that I wasn't sure what would happen next. She requested that we go upstate to visit him. I made all the arrangements to get time off from work, but we received last minute calls that the court dates had been postponed. Why couldn't they tell us sooner? I wasn't sure how much longer my job would allow me to take time off, only to cancel and then do it again. Didn't they realize that we had other children with special needs and it took tremendous effort to get ready for a trip like this?

Meanwhile, Chanel had been coming home from school in really high spirits. "What's up Chanel? I love this super mood you're in but what's behind all of this?"

She paused for a minute, then replied, "I hope you don't mind, but a boy in school asked me to go out with him. I like him a lot."

Wow, this was wonderful and frightening all at the same time.

"So tell me about him! What does he look like? Is he nice? How did you meet him?" These were all questions I needed to know. But most importantly, I wondered how mature he was. This was obviously good medicine for Chanel. She was so happy and in a better mood than usual. I loved this side of Chanel I had never seen before. I hoped she remembered our "birds and bees" talk!

On October 14, 2006, Alonna, Chanel and her date, Todd, attended the Home coming dance at 7:30 p.m. at the Pinellas Park High School. Alonna wore a very girly black lacy dress with a pearl necklace and matching pretty earrings. She put on her own makeup and pampered her hair. Chanel also chose a very pretty black dress, and shoes with mini heels. She wore no makeup. This would be Chanel's first date completely unsupervised by me. I wasn't sure Chanel was ready for the independence, and I could see that she wasn't sure as well. As we pulled into the packed parking lot, I saw several uniformed police officers keeping a

Alonna and Chanel

vigilant watch on things. The girls were nervous as I dropped the two of them off, with Chanel frantically looking around for familiar faces. I walked the girls to the door and spoke to a few of the chaperones that were there specifically for the ESE students. They assured me the girls would be fine. In the distance, I could see Todd dressed in a dress shirt and black slacks.

186

Later that evening when the girls were safely back home, Chanel whispered to me, "I had my very first dance and my very first kiss tonight, Mom."

"Ugh, I'm not ready for this," I thought. For the next few days I could hear giggling from their rooms as Alonna and Chanel exchanged secrets. Chanel was so desperate to have a relationship like all the other high school students. In the last year or so she had several boyfriends but the relationships never lasted for more than a few days or so. When you have a daughter with special needs, they usually attract boys with special needs. This could be a problem because then the behavior issues were multiplied.

Over the past few years Chanel had become more and more adamant about getting what she wanted. She simply wouldn't accept "no" as an answer, asking for the same thing over and over, hoping to get our approval for whatever she wanted in that moment. She ignored all the structured limitations we set for her, eventually giving us no other choice but to put her in "time out." Sending her to her room for a period of time had usually worked in the past, but now the arguments between us lasted a full day and sometimes more. When I told my friends about what was going on, some would say things like, "Well, you must be giving into her at times or she wouldn't keep asking."

Armando and I had been Chanel's external brain for many years, as she was often unable to make good decisions on her own. Around the time of the dance, there was an incident that led us to take away Chanel's cell phone, radio and television privileges. She has asked me not to go into detail about this incident in the book. Another day she twisted my arm in anger because I wouldn't let her walk to a neighbor's home by herself. That was the one and only time she ever used physical means to try to get her way and has not had an outburst like that since. Overall, I must say I am happy with how Armando and I have handled Chanel's behavior issues. Although there is no permanent fix, we have seen that with the right strategies the stress load can be somewhat lightened.

On October 19, 2006, we received another call to arrange for a visit with Trent and, this time no one called to cancel. The other supervisors at my job had been most helpful in allowing me to prepare the FMLA and medical leave request and covered my shifts while I was away. They all wished us well as we got ready to depart for the long drive to upstate New York. Most of our things were already packed from the last two visits that had been cancelled. We sang our usual silly songs all the way there. Rosina was so excited her voice crackled when she attempted to sing. "Mommy, I can't wait to see my brother, Oh my God, I'm so excited! Hurry up, let's get there!"

We arrived at 2:00 a.m., to an area of New York that was very unfamiliar to us. We hadn't booked a hotel reservation due to lack of time and we were having trouble finding somewhere to stay. Finally Chanel called out, "Mom, look there's a big parking lot, why can't we just park there for a few hours until we can get in to see Trent?" So that's exactly what we did. Chanel had noticed that there were many police cars in the parking lot, it was well lit, and there was barbed wire surrounding the building. That made it feel like a safe place to park. We had no idea what the building was. None of us were able to rest since we were filled with ex-

citement and on high alert in this unfamiliar territory. Later that morning, but still too early for visiting hours, we left the parking lot and drove to a diner where we sat for an hour or so. After asking a few people for directions to St. Mary's one man pointed out several hotels in the area. We told him we had been resting in that big parking lot up the street, since it was so well lit. The man started laughing, "That's Sing Sing!" To this date we all laugh about spending the night at the famous maximum security prison, especially Rosina. She was so quick to tell everyone, "We were at SING SING."

As the night turned to day, we finally headed out for St. Mary's. It was just a matter of time for all of us to see Trent's beautiful little face for the first

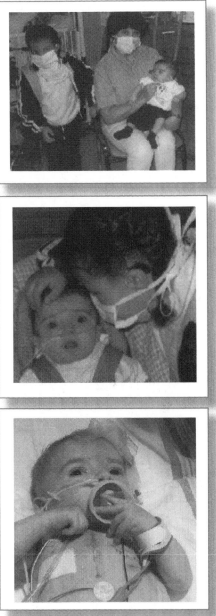

Rosina meets her bio brother, Trent (Antonio), for the first time

time. St. Mary's was nestled on a large and peaceful picturesque lot, with the rehabilitation center and hospital situated high up on a hill and surrounded by many tall trees.

We had no idea what Trent looked like or if he was Caucasian. We didn't ask because it didn't matter to any of us. As we entered the front door we went straight to a small welcome window and inquired about little Trent. The receptionist asked to see proof of our identification, then said, "We've been waiting for you," as she escorted us to Trent's room. She asked each of us to put on a mask for Trent's protection, and then she pushed the door open and waved us in. There were three children in the room, we weren't sure which one was Trent.

Then Rosina yelled out, "Mommy, come look! I think this one is him! Look, it has his name on the toys."

We all stared at Trent, and he looked just as hard back at us. Although his face was somewhat robust, there was a very noticeable blue hue to his complexion, nasogastric tubing entered one of his nares, and oxygen tubing was taped to the side of his face. He wasn't at all afraid of us and just loved the multitude of attention. The Torres family was able to spend the whole day with him, holding him, playing peek-a-boo, even reading a story to him. Chanel was the most hesitant to hold him. I think all the tubing concerned her. She went to each baby in the room talking to them and handing them a toy that was at the foot of their crib. Rosina didn't leave Trent's side. All the nurses were wonderful. Trent was quite the popular little guy and everyone knew him.

An overwhelmingly empty sad feeling flowed over me as the

day once again turned to night knowing the time was nearing for us to leave. It was time to say goodbye to this little boy, a little boy I hardly knew. I hated leaving him behind. I don't think he understood what I said, but I promised I'd fight hard to bring him to our home. Each of us kissed him on the forehead and we left. It broke my heart to leave Trent behind as we drove to Long Island. We visited with my daughters Alexa and Dana and, of course, our Jayne Avenue friends and neighbors. Then we started our long drive back to Florida.

From November 10-13, 2006, Armando and Jessica were in Antigua for Dana's wedding. They left early in the morning. Once again I was missing out on another special family day due to my extreme fear of flying.

My adult daughters reminded me again, "There are things you can do to get rid of those fears, Mom! "

"But why, I like these fears and I don't EVER want to fly!" I replied.

Chanel and Dana had been best buddy sisters for many years and the connection between these two was adorable. Chanel begged to be able to fly to Antigua with Armando but I was too worried about her being in a strange place. Besides I wanted Armando to be able to focus on Dana getting married, without the pressure of monitoring Chanel's every move.

November 16, 2006 was little Trent's first birthday. We sent a large package of gifts and clothes to St. Mary's. We wished we could spend the special day with him. If he only knew how very hard we were working to get him adopted and have him come live with the Torres family in Florida.

Each year my adult daughters and I would take turns hosting the family Christmas party, and in 2006 Trudy and Carlos were more than happy to welcome all of us, including Chanel's boyfriend Todd, to their home for a Christmas Eve gathering. Christmas food, gifts, fun, laughs and hugs were all just an hour away. There was nothing like the Torres family when we were all together. I have read horror stories of other families at holiday time, but for us, this was a time to strengthen family bonds. We were so blessed to have each other and truly loved these family gatherings and being together. As we entered Trudy's home I immediately got that warm and fuzzy Christmas feeling as Trudy and the grandchildren greeted us at the door, with the smell of delicious food filling the air. The Christmas tree was lit, and the home was filled with Santa decorations and lots of other Christmas decor. Trudy's mother-in-law Marta was there, a gentle and kind woman in her 50s. She was very quiet that night, not her usual bubbly, happy self. We were all aware of her cancer diagnosis, but she had already surpassed her doctor's predictions. The evening was moving along wonderfully. Chanel sat right next to Marta on the sofa, while her boyfriend Todd talked to several guests in another room. Chanel and Marta began to talk, but not for long. Soon I heard lots of commotion from that direction, and when I looked over, I saw that Chanel was having a seizure. She was thrashing wildly and her lips were becoming cyanotic, (turning blue from lack of oxygen). She was choking. Her head and arms hit the hard tile floor with a cracking loud thud as she slid off the sofa and onto the floor. I don't know how she avoided fracturing a bone. Marta was doing her best to comfort Chanel; stroking Chanel's head and hand as she looked on in horror. Someone called the paramedics, and Chanel was transported to Mease Country-side Hospital where we spent the majority of Christmas Eve. At first I had no clue what triggered this pseudo-seizure. Stress had always preceded her seizures, but she hadn't had one in many months. Why this night on Christmas Eve and in front of sweet Marta, who had her own worries? Later in the week, Chanel told me more about what had happened, though she has asked me not to write in detail about it in this book and she will have final approval before the book is released.

Right before the Christmas Eve dinner, Chanel's boyfriend Todd had been pressuring her into something she was adamant about not doing. She stuck to her beliefs, something Dr. Cimino had talked to her about many years ago. I was so proud of Chanel for coming to me for help and asked her to come to me sooner before the stress builds up into a seizure.

It was that time of year once again when Armando and I tally up the list of items broken by Chanel: two more television sets, several remote controls, the toaster, more glasses and dishes, the washing machine, the overhead fan in her room, the covers to several DVD's, zippers on two back packs and on a sweater, a small cement figurine in the front yard, and once again the list was long. We had started praising Chanel at the end of the day if she had gotten through a day without breaking something. We found this advice online from psychologist Julius Segal of the American Psychological Association: "Praise a child's achievements; let them know you have noticed how they gently placed a toy back where it belonged after playing with it." He explained, "Children will feed off the cheering and learn to treat their belongings and others with care." We learned to take whatever advice we could get, and shared tips back and forth with other adoptive families of children with fetal alcohol syndrome who had the very same concerns.

Sadly, Marta died at 10:00 a.m. on January 17, 2007, with her family at her side. I reflected back on that awful Christmas Eve, and how gently Marta had tried to comfort Chanel as she thrashed wildly out of control. Marta would be missed.

From March 22-26, 2007, I was left behind again as Armando went to New York to celebrate Alexa's honor roll induction. The girls were older now and able to help me more than they had in the past when Armando was away. But I never let my guard down with Chanel, I was always ready for the unexpected.

On April 29, 2007, I happily called out, "Get in the car, Chanel, c'mon, I'm taking you someplace."

Chanel had a perplexed look on her face as we pulled up to Pet Land, in Largo. Just as soon as we walked through the door I looked towards the back of the store and saw a perfect dog for Chanel. There was a six-month-old Italian greyhound, a small breed that Chanel would be able to lift easily. On our drive home, Chanel received lots of kisses from our new little one, who she decided to name ELIZABETH TAYLOR! From this day forward, Elizabeth became Chanel's trusted confidant and knew all her innermost secrets. Chanel was madly in love with her new dog and they quickly became best friends. This kept Chanel out of trouble for a few weeks, anyway.

By the end of the next month, Elizabeth Taylor was developing into a wonderful, entertaining and loyal companion for Chanel. As with all puppies, caring for Elizabeth was a huge responsibility and served as a bigger purpose for Chanel than even she could imagine. Like most young people, she figured all a dog needed was food, water and love. She was abruptly finding out there was way more responsibility in raising a puppy. We enrolled Elizabeth in puppy classes at PetSmart, where Chanel and I would take her twice a week for several weeks. Chanel loved when it was her turn to bring Elizabeth to the center of the ring.

At home, we were still working out a few details. After a few doggy incontinent accidents right by the front door, we had no choice but to crate Elizabeth Taylor during the night until Chanel would walk her in the morning. During the week things were fine because Chanel was up early for school. On the weekends, though Chanel wanted to sleep until 10:00 a.m. After a few weeks of arguing about the doggy incontinent accidents, I threatened to find the pooch a new home, Chanel finally understood that she would have to get up earlier, even on the weekends.

On June 29, 2007, we had a 2:30 p.m. appointment with Dr. Chaves, after Chanel complained of pain in her left shoulder area. After a full examination Dr. Chavez found four tumor-like projections at the supra-clavicular area of her neck/shoulder. He referred her to the general pediatric surgical group.

Armando and I quickly make plans to take the family on another trip to Disney World prior to our appointment with the general surgeon. Our grandson, BoDean, and the girls got ready for the trip, we didn't speak at all about Chanel's shoulder problems.

As per Dr. Chave'z request, on July 18, 2007 we saw Dr. Fairchild at All Children's Hospital. He was also concerned about the hard raised areas on Chanel's left shoulder and wanted to do a biopsy. We scheduled an appointment for the biopsy about two weeks later.

On July 30, 2007, Chanel and I arrived at All Children's Hospital with knots in our stomachs. At 10:00 a.m. she was placed under general anesthesia for a biopsy of the tumor that was palpable and very prominent on her left clavicular area. Much sooner than expected, Dr. Fairchild came out to the waiting room. He was there to tell me he was unable to complete the biopsy because the tumor was a very rare and hard form. We were discharged the next day with instructions to follow up with him on August 21, 2007. I prayed the stress Chanel was enduring would not trigger a pseudo seizure.

Our follow up appointment on August 21, 2007 was devastating, though I did my best not to break down in front of Chanel. As he examined Chanel's shoulder Dr. Fairchild noticed a rather large "café au lait" spot on her left shoulder. He told us the tumors were possibly a form of neurofibromatosis, and needed further follow up.

"Oh my God, did he just say what I thought he said?" I was so crushed I wanted to cry! The first thing that popped into my head was the elephant man disease. My beautiful baby, my beautiful Chanel! My body went limp but I remained expressionless. The news hit me hard, like a ton of bricks had just fallen on my head, but I had to remain calm for Chanel. As I looked at her flat affect and blank expression, I knew she was confused and uncertain, I wasn't sure she fully understood what Dr. Fairchild was telling us. I wondered what she must be thinking. I realized she had no clue what neurofibromatosis was. I didn't want to alarm her so I didn't make eye contact for the rest of the visit. What's next? I wondered, she has already been through the wringer! Dr. Fairchild instructed us to follow up with genetics and the neurosurgeon Dr. Mullen.

We saw Dr. Mullen on August 23, 2007 at 4:30 p.m., and set an appointment for yet another biopsy.

The doctor's diagnosis of neurofibromatosis kept ringing in my head, and at this point my goal was to make Chanel happy-to buy her whatever she wanted and, take her wherever she wanted go. One of Chanel's favorite places to shop was at Pet Smart. So on September 2, 2007 we drove there to pick up some things for her pets. As we pulled up, we saw three or four large greyhounds that were up for adoption. Chanel leaped from the car, all excited, and begins to run across the parking lot toward the dogs, begging me to adopt one before she could even reach the dogs. She didn't have to beg for long. We adopted Sir Richard Burton who was a three-year-old retired racing greyhound. Now we had Elizabeth Taylor the mini (Italian) greyhound and Sir Richard Burton. As I said, at this time I was giving Chanel pretty much whatever she wanted. Unfortunately, Richard Burton and Elizabeth Taylor didn't get along so after eight weeks they got divorced and we had to return Richard back to the greyhound rescue group. Chanel was very protective of Elizabeth so she wasn't very upset when we had to return Richard.

On September 5, 2007, Chanel had an MRI of her shoulder at All Children's Hospital at the request of the neurosurgeon.

A few days later we attended Chanel's IEP (individualized education program) meeting at Pinellas Park High School. With the possibility of neurofibromatosis weighing heavily on our minds, Chanel and I were both very quiet at this meeting, finding it hard to contribute or communicate with staff. At the end of the meeting Chanel told the teachers her doctor thought she had neurofibromatosis, although further testing needed to be done. Things suddenly got very quiet; I could hear slight noises in the very far distance. All the teachers agreed to take it easy on Chanel and play it by ear.

Soon after that, Dana arrived in Florida for a visit, the timing was perfect. Chanel needed Dana's emotional support. The fear of the unknown was tearing us up. Right after Dana returned to New York, Chanel was back in the operating room at All Children's Hospital with Dr. Mullen. I waited nervously in the conference room for Dr. Mullen to come and give me a report.

As soon as I saw him entering the room I stood up. I didn't like the expression on his face and almost told him "I don't want to hear this," but of course I didn't say a word. I needed to know what the biopsy revealed so we could make a plan of care. Dr.

Mullen was a big man. As I sat back down, he towered over me and leaned on the back wall wearing a somewhat perplexed look on his face.

"Mrs. Torres, I have good news and I have bad news." That didn't make a bit of sense to me what-so-ever. He continued to say, "The good news is, Chanel doesn't have neurofibromatosis."

Wow, powerful stuff, but if this was the good news what could the bad news be?

"Chanel has an extra rib, it's called a cervical rib; it split into four and the brachial plexus nerve bundle has wrapped itself around the rib."

He explained that a cervical rib is a congenital condition. Often it's not diagnosed until adolescence when symptoms begin, as was the case with Chanel. "Any injury to the nerve bundle could cause paralysis in that arm or diminished use. Even feather light touching of the nerve could be detrimental. If Chanel continues to complain of severe pain we could attempt to remove the rib."

I was just sick to my stomach. Oh my God, here we go again! Chanel has been reporting her pain level as being 10 out of 10 for weeks now. She had taken powerful pain medication to no avail. I didn't know what to do or where to turn. At this point Dr. Mullen started Chanel on Neurontin and Amitriptyline HCL (Amitriptyline HCL is usually used for depression, but for Chanel, it was being used synergistically with Neurontin for pain) along with instructions to return for a follow-up appointment in a few weeks. He also suggested we make an appointment with the genetics department. The ride home was quiet. Chanel wasn't asking very many questions at this point. We didn't know if we should be happy she didn't have neurofibromatosis or not.

We saw a geneticist on November 8, 2007, and after a lengthy physical examination and lab tests, she confirmed that Chanel did not have neurofibromatosis. YEAH!

We had been waiting for this letter for a very long time, and on November 15, 2007 it arrived. I couldn't wait to read it to Rosina. After so many false alarms of promised adoption dates, we finally had a date secured.

PRESS RELEASE

Court to Give Kids the Gift of

Family on Adoption Friday

Central Islip, N.Y. – On Friday, December 7, 2007, the Suffolk County Family Court, located in the Co-halan Court Complex, Central Islip, New York, will be holding its 7th annual "adoption Friday"- a spe-cial adoption day when the family court will expedite cases to make the upcoming holiday season extra special for as many children and their adoptive par-ents as possible.

The Honorable David Freundlich, Supervising Judge of the Suffolk County Family Court, will be presiding and his court will be open for business at 8:00 a.m. to facilitate the extra cases.

According to Judge Freundlich, "Our Family Court staff does a wonderful job year round in expediting adoptions but they all take pride at this time of the year in extending themselves to have an "Adoption Friday" which is extra special for almost four times the number of families than we usually have."

"Adoptions are one of the happiest and most satisfying proceedings we have in the Suffolk County courts," said District Administrative Judge H. Patrick Leis 111. "As we head towards the holiday season, I am especially grateful to Judge Freundlich, his staff and our Family Court personnel for their hard work and very special efforts in making "adoption Friday" a reality."

The weather was perfect on December 1, 2007, as our family excitedly piled into the car and headed out for the Islip Cohalan family court building once again. We left Florida before the sunrise in the wee hours of the morning, while the roads were still quiet. We drove straight to upstate New York, arriving just before dawn on December 2nd. As soon as the sun beamed over the mountains, the Torres family once again got to visit Trent. His adoption day was set for December 7th, though Trent (soon to become Antonio) would not be able to attend the adoption ceremony because, he was too fragile. The nurses handed us many papers to sign and gave us instructions on feeding him through his newly placed Mic-key feeding button, (his nasogastric tube had been discontinued) then they shared a brief history about his special needs.

Armando and Rosina,
(Antonio-Trent's
biological sister)
at Antonio's adoption
December 7, 2007.

On December 7, 2007, we arrived at the Cohalan building early. Trent remained at St. Mary's, unfortunately missing out on the glorious ceremony due to his doctor's orders. Once again, we were called into closed chambers as we had been several times before. Rosina was beyond excited and could hardly contain her screams of happiness. We took lots of pictures so we could show Trent when he got older. We sat down at the same long desk, sitting beside the judge as he gave us many papers to sign.

Trent was now Antonio!

We had arranged for Susan T., an ARNP who knew him well from his cardiology team in New York, to fly him to us in Florida on December 10th. This gave us just enough time to drive back home, arriving on the 9th. We were all excited for little Antonio's arrival the next day. We had already arranged for

Antonio at
Christmas time
with new family.

all of his oxygen needs and other supplies, so there was not much to do but wait.

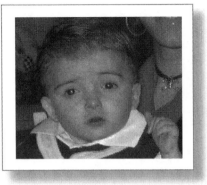

Antonio

December 10th, 2007, Antonio arrived in his new home in Florida via Continental Airline at 1:20 p.m. Susan the ARNP reported that keeping his oxygen flowing properly during the flight was much more difficult than she had anticipated. They looked exhausted.

Antonio was dressed in the cutest outfit, something that Susan had bought for him. When they arrived, the girls were sitting on the floor. When Susan put Antonio down, he immediately crawled straight to Rosina, who, of course, had the biggest smile on her face. Susan visited for a few hours before heading back to New York. We were now a family of eleven and extremely grateful to Susan.

CHAPTER TWENTY-TWO:

CHANEL'S NEW CAREER

In January 2008, Chanel was a high school senior. One day she jumped off the school bus, bolted across the lawn, and almost tripped as she burst into the house, flinging the door open with so much force that it banged the wall behind it. In a very rushed and excited tone, she said, "Sit down, Mom, I want to talk to you, Mrs. Luisi from Pinellas Park High School would like me to speak to her class about my diagnosis of fetal alcohol syndrome." Chanel was having an extremely difficult time with her speech fluency at this time, plus she was out of breath from the sprint across the lawn. Her stuttering had worsened over the past few months and students from her school often made fun of her by giggling, whispering and pointing at her in halls. This was devastating for Chanel. All I could imagine was Chanel standing up in front of the class and not being able to spit out a single word, followed by laughter from the students. I did my best to keep my thoughts positive, but I couldn't help but wonder, "What is this teacher thinking? Chanel could hardly get out two consecutive words! How in the world would she be able to speak to a class full of students?" I nodded and smiled, then said, that's nice." The conversation consumed my thoughts for the rest of the evening, as I hoped the idea would just go away. The next day I asked Chanel how she felt about speaking in front of the class. "I visited my speech teacher Mrs. Sargent today and she's going to start training me for public speaking." She hurriedly yelled out her words, which were all scrambled together.

Hmm, okay, I truly didn't think Chanel could do this and I really didn't want her to get hurt. But I also didn't want to discourage her, if this was what she wanted to do. I had to hide my true feelings.

Over the next few months I watched as Chanel spent a great deal of her time researching fetal alcohol syndrome. She browsed internet websites and pages, as always, but her primary source of information was now YouTube. Her reading skills were still several levels behind, and she learned better from listening and watching rather than reading. I loved when she would run into my room with excitement to tell me something she had just learned about fetal alcohol syndrome, and it was often something I was learning for the first time as well. She knew more about fetal alcohol syndrome than most doctors did, as she would tell me.

"I live with it every day, Mom, I understand it well!"

In February, 2008, after only one week of extensive speech

therapy, Chanel had her first speaking engagement, a five minute presentation in front of a small group of students. Her anxiety level was at an all-time high. Public speaking creates stress and anxiety for many people and Chanel was certainly no exception. When her anxiety level was high she had the propensity to stutter more than usual; her body would tremble and her hands would shake.

At home, I waited eagerly for Chanel to come home from school and tell me all about her day and her speech. When I heard the bus coming up the street, I ran to the door and waited for her. As I watched her getting off the bus, I couldn't read her expression as I usually could.

"Hurry, Chanel," I called out, "Come tell me all about your day. How did it go?"

"It was okay," she replied, in a sad tone.

"What do you mean? Were you nervous? How many people were there? Tell me everything! I want to know, I'm so excited for you!"

"Yes, I was very nervous," said Chanel, "and my stuttering was bad but it was only a five-minute speech. I guess it was okay. Everyone said they liked it and that they didn't know I had fetal alcohol syndrome"

"I'm so proud of you Chanel," I exclaimed, "You sure are brave!" I knew that most people would have been discouraged at this point, and given up on the idea of public speaking. I tentatively asked, "Do you think you will do this again?"

"I think so," she replied," But I'm not sure yet." My teacher is already talking about booking me for other classes."

On March 12, 2008, Antonio was scheduled at 7:00 a.m. for yet another open-heart surgery, this time it will be done at All Children's Hospital.

Chanel awoke early to wish Antonio well and see us off before we left for the hospital. She shared that she might be doing another speech that day for another group of students. Of course I badly wanted to be with her, but this was Antonio's first open-heart surgery in Florida. He'd already had

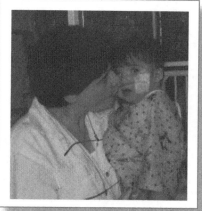

Antonio just before his open heart surgery in Florida

three open heart surgeries prior to adoption. His oxygen saturations were ranging from 68-74% on 3-4 liters of oxygen and he had generalized cyanoses. He was given a 70% chance of NOT making it through the surgery.

After the surgery, he had to stay in the cardiovascular intensive care unit and of course I stayed right by his side, watching his every move. At one point, I asked one of the nurses to keep an eye on him, explaining that I had to make an important phone call.

I rushed off the CVICU unit and into an area with good cell phone reception.

"Hi, Chanel," I said, "How did your speech go?"

"Better than last time," she said.

"Wow, I am so very proud of you, next time I would love to

be there! Please let me know so I can work my schedule around your next speech."

After a short conversation with Chanel, I remained with Antonio until his discharge day on April 4th, only to return again on April 15th with an elevated temperature until he was discharged again on April 17th. Once again, on April 18th we were back in the ER because Antonio had not voided in a long time. This time, we were sent home, only to return again on the 19th, when he was admitted to the PICU and remained until April 23rd. It was an extremely difficult and exhausting month for us, between the back and forth trips to the hospital and making sure that either Armando or I were at home with Chanel at all times when she wasn't in school. Chanel was mostly supportive through it all, and even though I missed yet another one of her speeches, she was very understanding.

June 3, 2008, Chanel graduated from Pinellas Park High School. The ceremony was held at Ruth Eckerd Hall in Clearwater. It was such a glorious day. Chanel was as proud of herself as we all were, since she had read on many different web sites that many students with fetal alcohol syndrome do not graduate from high school. Chanel had endured the taunting of students and bullies from middle school all the way through high school.

They had pegged her as "different." This bullying only added to her stress and anxiety level. Other ESE students had similar experiences. For this reason, Chanel left a legacy for future students. The "Class Train" was something that Chanel and her friend April created in order to avoid being singled out by bullies. The ESE students had discovered that if they stuck together, they were stronger in numbers. So as they traveled to their special class, they formed a line (train style) and took turns being the conductor. To avoid being bullied in the cafeteria, Chanel and other ESE students ate together in the classroom.

From July 5-10, 2008, Rosina was the special guest on a six-day Disney cruise to Nassau, Bahamas, courtesy of the Make-a-Wish foundation. Our whole family got to go and we even got special permission to include my grandson, BoDean.

Rosina

Rosina on her Make a Wish Cruise

Everyone was up bright and early, our luggage was lined up neatly at the curb, along with Antonio's special supplies; IV pole, medications, formula, diapers, nebulizer equipment and much more. Rosina screamed with joy as the limousine pulled up to our house to deliver us to our destination of Port Canav-

Rosina, Armando, Chanel, Native Bahamian & BoDean

Alonna   Chanel & Alonna

eral. It was a vacation we would never forget, and the Make-A-Wish Foundation made sure Rosina was treated like a special little princess! It was a bonding experience for our whole family. During the cruise Alonna and Chanel wanted more freedom than I felt comfortable giving them. I knew I had to let them experience some time away from me. Chanel is a high school graduate!

I reminded myself! The ship seemed like a safe place to try this, so with a promise from both Chanel and Alonna that they would stay close to each other, off they went to explore the ship without Mom or Dad right at their side.

"Don't worry Mom, I have her back," Alonna yelled out to us. After going out for their second adventure, they returned to their staterooms whispering lots of secrets back and forth, both of them looked very concerned. Later that day, Chanel told me she was overwhelmed and wanted to stay with us from then on. To this day I don't know exactly what or who it was on that ship that frightened them.

After her graduation from Pinellas Park High School in Largo in 2008, Chanel started at the Pinellas Technical Education Center (PTEC) where she took general studies as an extended ESE student. What she enjoyed most was her computer class, where she was highly motivated to get started. With the help of her teacher, she excelled in this class and used the technology to further her research on fetal alcohol syndrome. This gave her the independence she needed and unlocked the future for her in many areas.

Chanel was gaining exponential speed in research in her speeches on the computer, giving her the confidence to speak with the most up to date information on the subject of fetal alcohol syndrome.

On October 20, 2008 at 2:00 p.m. she gave a presentation about fetal alcohol syndrome at the Pinellas Park High School for a Grade 12 child psychology class. This time I didn't miss her speech. I sat in the back so I wouldn't distract Chanel. I watched the students come into the classroom one by one. Most looked tired and uninterested in what Chanel had to say. Some plopped down into their seats and dropped their book bags onto the floor, others rested their heads on their desk with their eyes closed, completely tuning her out. About five minutes into the speech, Chanel began to speak of her personal struggles while living with fetal alcohol syndrome. All of a sudden, heads lifted up, backs

Chanel talking to a group of students at Pinellas Park High School about FAS

straightened, and as she continued I even noticed some of the students tearing up. They were listening intently to everything she had to say. Chanel was very good at interacting with the audience, and she asked them, "What do you think would happen if someone saw a very pregnant woman drinking a beer in public?" There was an enthusiastic response as many of the students raised their hands and offered answers. Chanel proceeded to tell them, "Nothing, nothing would happen because there isn't a law that prevents a pregnant woman from giving her baby beer while it's in utero"

The room was quiet, "If there was such a law that protected babies in utero, then maybe it would have stopped my birth mom from drinking and I wouldn't have to deal with the everyday struggles of fetal alcohol syndrome." She continued, "Now, what do you think would happen if someone saw a mom snap open a can of beer, fill up a baby bottle and give the beer to the baby to drink?"

Again, many of the students raised their hands, eager to give their answers. After hearing from a few of them, Chanel said, "Hopefully someone would call child protective services and report the mom, the child would be put into foster care, and the mom would be charged with child abuse."

Chanel speaking
at Pinellas Park
High School about FAS

The students all nodded in agreement. "So, why is it not abuse if you give the baby beer before birth?" After her 45-minute speech, Chanel had an open question and answer session with the students. "NO HOLDS BARRED" she told them, "I'm prepared to answer any question."

One student asked if Chanel had a baby, would that baby be born with fetal alcohol syndrome. That question continues to come up just about every time she speaks to high school students. She was happy to tell them, "No, the only way to get fetal alcohol syndrome is if the birth mother drinks alcohol when she is pregnant, and I don't ever want to make someone suffer the way I do."

I could see that these presentation sessions were becoming more and more therapeutic for Chanel. After her session, the teacher referred her to another class and she quickly booked another speaking engagement for April 19th. I was there again to witness as Chanel spoke to a group of nursing students at Pinellas Technical Education Center. This group was very engaged and listened to every word Chanel had to say. As I watched her at the front of the class, I noticed how confident she had become, and saw how much she truly enjoyed doing these speeches. She was gleaming at the end of the speech as each of the student nurses congratulated her bravery.

On April 29, 2010 an important letter arrived from Chanel's high school. Chanel enthusiastically ran up to me and waved the letter back and forth at my face, all while jumping up and down and begging, "Read it, Mom, hurry, please read it to me. Can we go Mom? Please, can we go?

The note said:

> "WE WOULD LIKE TO HONOR ALL
>
> OF THE AMAZING WORK YOU DO
>
> BY INVITING YOU AND A GUEST TO ATTEND
>
> OUR ANNUAL VOLUNTEER BREAKFAST
>
> ON THURSDAY, APRIL 29, 2010
>
> FROM 7:45-9:30 AM IN THE MEDIA CENTER
>
> HERE AT PINELLAS PARK HIGH SCHOOL."

We arrived early in the morning for this honorable day, beginning with a well-organized breakfast feast. Chanel dressed as she usually did when she gave a presentation about fetal alcohol syndrome, in business attire with her hair in a nice neat bun secured to the back of her head. When they called her name to come up to the podium for a certificate of appreciation, many of her teachers gave her the high five and yelled out, "Nice job, Chanel!"

"Mom" she said to me, "I am just doing what I love, advocating for unborn babies, if I could save one baby I would be happy, If I save more, then that's the biggest reward!"

Chanel had another speaking engagement on May 20, 2010, which I helped her prepare for. She liked to write each speech so that it was geared to each individual audience, but any changes had to be subtle. As with most victims of fetal alcohol syndrome, Chanel didn't cope well with the change. If I changed too many consecutive words, Chanel would become upset with me, telling me this was confusing for her. Meanwhile, she was becoming a pro at making eye contact with her audience, and her voice was more persuasive and convincing. Although she still stuttered and at times it got pretty bad, she was able to continue as though the stuttering never happened. She was so much more comfortable in front of an audience.

In August 2010, it was time for Chanel to move from PTEC to Richard L Sanders School in Pinellas Park, where students with special needs learned the skills that were necessary to grow into successful adults. Chanel wasn't happy about this move. "Mom Richard L. Sanders isn't the right school for me." I explained to Chanel that the PTEC program no longer offered an ESE class so the move was inevitable.

From August 12-17, 2010, our family took our second Disney cruise to the Bahamas, thank you again to the Make-a-Wish foundation! This time, Antonio was the special guest.

While on the cruise ship Alonna and Chanel stayed with the family. They didn't do any roaming around like they did on the last cruise. Chanel often became quite overwhelmed in large groups.

On September 15, 2010, it was Chanel to the rescue again. Little Antonio hemorrhaged right here in our kitchen and lost a large volume of blood.

Chanel initiated the 911 call and instructed everyone to lock up the pets, "Get Antonio's face-sheet ready," she yelled out to Rosina, "and I will go to the street to flag them down," I was sick with fear for my little boy, who was bleeding from his eyes, nose, ears and mouth for an unknown reason. He was taken to All Children's Hospital. The paramedics asked Chanel to get in the ambulance while I followed in my car. While in the quiet of my car I reflected on how organized Chanel had always been in any emergency situation the Torres family faced. Chanel's adrenalin kicks in big time during family crises and believe me we have had many, way more than any other family I know. It's the repetition that keeps Chanel on track. The ambulance arrived at the ER before I did, and Chanel was right at Antonio's side answering questions that the ER team was throwing at her.

His lab results from last week's lab draw were within normal range. His hemoglobin was somewhat low. The platelet count was in the low-normal range, and today's lab results revealed the same results.

Antonio was admitted for observation and hematology started a workup on him. He was discharged two days later, but not for long because he suffered a slight case of epistaxis (nosebleed) and

I rushed him back to the ER for fear of a repeat of the full-blown hemorrhage. This would not be the end of his bleeding episodes, a third episode occurred. This time he was admitted to All Children's Hospital for a full work up.

I didn't get my break for several days, and then I was able to go home for a quick shower and spend a few minutes on Facebook to talk to friends. While I was on Facebook I poured my heart out in a post to my friends, telling them of my horrific last few days. Dr. Sprintzen posted a comment, telling me to have the hematologist look for Bernard Souliers syndrome, a rare bleeding disorder. This diagnosis was soon confirmed by the hematologist. Now we could add Bernard-Soulier syndrome to the list of issues he already had. With this disorder the platelet count can be in the normal range but the platelets themselves are large and do not support aggregation (clotting).

In November 2010, I took a family medical leave from work while Rosina had her second open-heart surgery to receive a prosthetic pulmonary valve. Chanel was once again supportive while the family was in crisis. She was so good at organizing things at home with the pets and helping Armando with Antonio. It was incredible to watch as Chanel matured into a young woman.

CHAPTER TWENTY-THREE:

THE SEARCH IS ON

I knew that at some point, Chanel would ask again about her biological family. It's a natural curiosity that all adopted children have. Every adoption comes with a fascinating history, however convoluted it may be. Several years earlier she had asked, "Where does Christine live? Why was I put up for adoption? Do I have any brothers or sisters? Who is my biological father?" I had answered her questions the best I could.

In September 2011, Chanel was asking all the same questions once again, but this time she was adamant about finding the answers. This was not just a fleeting thought. I could hear it in her voice. She was trying her best to be gentle with her questions, because she didn't want to hurt me. I was the one who wasn't mentally prepared for this. Chanel was the love of my life, and I wasn't sure I was ready to share her. I was forever grateful for the privilege of sharing our lives with this amazing young woman, Chanel.

"What if we find Christine," I thought "And she wants Chanel back in her life as if there had been no pause? What if she wants Chanel to call her, 'Mommy'?" Chanel was easily influenced and I knew she could be swayed to whatever Christine suggested. Meanwhile, Christine had no clue about the time and effort Armando and I had put into raising Chanel; all with great love, I might add.

Of course, Christine would say she appreciated the effort of raising her child. But this was different. With Chanel's diagnosis of fetal alcohol syndrome she requires at least three times as much parenting. How could I ever explain to her that Chanel took more compassion and intense parenting than my three other special needs children combined? How could I explain that the hidden disabilities and subtle challenges all added up to so—*SO MUCH MORE*. And could I do that in a loving way that did not cause shame to here.

I wanted Christine to be involved in Chanel's life, but from a distance. Christine was an important piece in the puzzle of Chanel's life and I knew she held several missing links, i.e., family history. She had given us some information in her notes many years back, but what else was there to know about her background and health issues? And was her time at the Charles K. Post rehab program successful? I knew that having Christine in our lives would bring gains and losses for each of us.

There were so many different thoughts flying around my head

at this moment. I was trying to be supportive because I knew how important this was to Chanel.

"One of my teachers offered to help me, Mom. She will help me find Christine," she continued to say. I assured her I would do my best to help with the search and I meant it sincerely. I wondered if Christine had been looking for Chanel. We hadn't heard from her since Chanel was about two and a half years old.

Chanel asked to see the letters Christine had left in her baby bag so many years ago. I told her I would show them to her as soon as I found them, as they were stored away for safe-keeping. Although I wasn't quite ready to share them with Chanel just yet, I made a promise to myself to find the letters and start the search for Christine.

Meanwhile, Chanel wrote this note to Christine then handed it to me for safe keeping, with the hope of giving all the notes to Christine sometime in the future:

Septembra 2011

Dear Christine

I have been reading a lot a bout FAS I want to teach people about it. I know that I have FAS u gave it to me. I don't know if I am mad at you. I know that I am mad that I have FAS. It's very hard to know that you give this to me. I won the local YES I CAN AWARD. I am still hoping to get to meet you someday. are u still in NY? I have something's to say to you. I hope that you would like to get to know me. I am trying to be good. I have been doing a lot of speeches this year about FAS. I hate having FAS. I have a lot of pets. I have a parrot, my dogs name is Elizabeth. I don't know if u know this but I don't live in NY anymore I life in FL. We moved here when I was 12 and now I am almost 22. Something's my Brain will tell my hands to do one thing and my hands will do something different when I write. I talk better then I write. I think it's the FAS. I am very good on the computer I take computers in school

From Chanel

Sometime in the month of October 2011, Chanel got a job working for an animal clinic through the school's career-based instructional training program, designed to prepare students with special needs for work in a regular setting, with the close guidance of a work counselor. The clinic was located right near her school. Soon after she arrived to school at 8:00 a.m. each morning, her teachers-aid would accompany her to the clinic then pick her up at 12:00 noon. Each afternoon, Chanel came home filled with all the great stories of the day. This was her dream job and she was on cloud nine with excitement! Chanel was so very dedicated to this job. The clinic technicians were training her to become a kennel tech.

Chanel had bonded with some of the animals, and easily became over-attached. When they got sick Chanel cried herself to sleep. As time went on, Chanel was finding it harder and harder to follow the many instructions she was given in a day. The tasks weren't complicated, but some of them required, five or more steps. And each day there were new instructions, completely different from the day before, something Chanel struggled with. She needed consistency and repetition. The strain was showing. She was forgetting to clean out the dog cages, forgetting to feed the pets or giving some too much food or not enough. She wasn't letting the dogs out into the clinic yard to empty their bladder.

At one point when we were in the waiting room of the All Children's Hospital ER with Antonio, Chanel jumped up and asked for my cell phone. She ran outside and called work, and when she came back she was crying. She had forgotten to feed a diabetic cat!

I could see that the pressure of this job was taking a toll on her; she lost weight, had dark circles under her eyes and was utterly stressed out. Amazingly, the job lasted for almost one full year.

Three weeks after the cat incident, Chanel arrived at work and saw her job coach speaking to Anna, the kennel tech supervisor. This really concerned her because the job coach only came to her job when there was a problem. Chanel had just punched in her time card when Anna came up to her and said in a sad yet serious tone:

"Come with me, I need to talk to you." Chanel, the job coach and Anna were now standing in one of the examining rooms. Chanel was leaning up against the wall, trying to hold her body still and keep it from trembling. Chanel remembers those devastating words, *"It isn't working out, Chanel."*

She felt her knees buckle out from under her, and she was now squatting down close to the floor. Chanel was in shock, and felt very hurt. She loved this job with all her heart! She left the room to collect a few of her belongings from her assigned cubby compartment. On her way out she was able to quickly run back and say good-bye to Sary and Bruce, two of her favorite patients.

The job coach asked Chanel to get in the car so he could drive her home. During the drive home, Chanel continued to cry and felt '*low and hurt*' by the job coach's stinging words. "You had the easiest job, Chanel," he said, "and you couldn't do it."

Chanel cupped her face in her hands and cried uncontrollably.

Meanwhile, I had promised her that I would help find her family, so we moved on to something new.

January 4, 2012 I had located the box of letters that Christine wrote many years ago. I sifted through the box alone in secret, wanting to read the letters to myself once again. The last time I read these letters was when Chanel was about seven years old, so this was like reading them for the first time.

Christine had written about much of her family history. Most importantly, she had included the names and birthdates of family members, along with the towns where I might find them. The letter that especially got to me was the one where she wrote about signing the adoption papers:

> *"I am **signing** the adoption papers today*
> **with a heavy hand and heart."**
> **Love Mommy**

I got goose bumps when I read this letter, as if I had never read it before. This time I stored the pile of letters under my mattress, for easier access.

Whenever I need to talk to someone who understands what I am going through I call Carolee, one of my New York friends and the adoptive mother of two children with special needs. "No, No Sondra!" she exclaimed you can't leave the letters under the mattress, she will find them."

I assure Carolee, "There was no way she will find them; she would have no reason to be looking under my mattress!"

I spent the rest of that day on the phone looking for Chanel's sister, Susan. One by one I was told, "Sorry, honey, you have the wrong people, we don't know a Susan B." As dusk approached I decided to stop and call the last two numbers in the morning. But as the evening progressed, it was still on my mind and I decided to make the call. It was a bit late but I just couldn't wait until the morning.

"Hello my name is Sondra;" I started the call just as I had all the others, "I'm the adoptive mother of Chanel, previously known as Elizabeth B. I believe Susan B. is her sister. Do you know of a Susan B.?" I heard a soft gasp followed by a cough on the other end of the phone. "So you do know Susan B.?" I asked.

The woman replied, "This is Judy and yes, I do know Susan." She hesitated to give me any information at this point, but acknowledged that yes, she was aware that Susan had a sister who was adopted out to someone.

Judy promised to talk to Michael, Susan's father, that night and asked me to call Michael the following night at 7:00 p.m.

Chanel had begun to suspect that I was up to something. She had been coming into my room more frequently the past few days. When I asked her what she wanted she always came up with an answer that made no sense whatsoever. As I was making my phone calls, several times I could see Chanel's feet under the door, as she listened in on my conversations. So I started bringing the phone into the bathroom and locking the door.

I still hadn't said a word to Chanel. I wanted to make sure we had the right people and that Susan B. wanted to talk to Chanel. I knew nothing about this woman, other then what her mother Christine wrote in a note many years ago. She had included Susan's full name (omitted here to protect her privacy), date of birth, the state and town where she lived and the fact that Susan had received a full scholarship to the University of Syracuse and wanted to become a veterinarian. I was so excited after speaking to Judy that it was hard not to run to Chanel and just blurt out, "I think I found your family." Keeping a secret of this magnitude was nearly impossible. My willpower was in overdrive.

Before I could call Michael at 7:00 p.m. on January 5, 2012, he called me on my cell phone at 2:00 p.m. as I was sitting in my recliner chair next to my bed. When I saw the name on my caller

ID I was both excited and nervous.

Michael started the conversation with a tone of skepticism as he proceeded to ask, "How do I know you are who you say you are and not some weirdo?"

"I understand your skepticism, Michael," I assured him, "Why don't I read some of the letters Christine wrote to me many years ago? Would that help you in knowing that I am the adoptive mother of Chanel?" I didn't even give him a chance to answer, I just began to tell him what I knew about Susan, and about Christine's alcohol problem as well as a few other things I remembered from the letters. About halfway through our 40-minute call, Michael began to relax and started to give me some information about Christine. He seemed to trust me at this point and our conversation was going more smoothly. It was then that Michael told me Christine had died from a fall in her apartment on January 21, 1995. My heart just plopped to the floor. I couldn't believe what Michael had just told me. Gosh, in 1995 Christine was only 42 years old and this was just a few years after we had adopted Chanel. I knew Chanel would be devastated to hear this news.

"Susan went to clean the apartment after her mother's death," he continued. As we closed our conversation Michael told me he would get in touch with Susan and have her call Chanel. I thanked him and we hung up.

Chanel never had a relationship with Christine, except for about two and half years when she was in our foster care prior to the adoption. But she had written letters to Christine through the years. Chanel always wanted to tell her about the wonderful things that had been happening in her life and the not so wonderful things as well. Now that could never happen.

I still didn't mention any of this to Chanel. I wanted to make sure Susan wanted a relationship with her sister.

Keeping this secret was very hard. Every time I saw Chanel I wanted to give her a big hug and tell her everything I had found out from Michael.

On January 6, 2012, I began the search for Robert F.H., Chanel's father. I checked Google, Facebook and Classmates. com. I found several Robert's with the same last name, jotted them down and then called the operator for the phone numbers. I called each number and spoke to some really nice people who sincerely wanted to help me, but they had no clue who Robert was. As I continued down the list of numbers, I left a message for a woman by the name of Virginia, telling her I was looking for Robert. "If you know him, could you please give him my phone number and ask him to call me?" Virginia's name had come up as a possible relative of Robert's.

Then onto the next phone number, and this time a man answered and happily told me, "Yes, I'm Robert F.H."

"Did you say you were Robert F.H.?"

"Yes, yes, I'm Robert, how can I help you?"

"I believe I adopted a child you fathered."

Robert sounded really upset, saying, "No, no, I don't have any children and I don't know any Christine!" and then he hung up on me. Several hours later, I called Chanel into my room and gently explained to her what I had been up to. About 15 minutes into our conversation my cell phone rang. I quickly looked at the caller ID and noticed it was the Robert I had just been speaking to. I was at a loss at what to tell Chanel, who was still standing right next to me.

"It's Robert," I said to Chanel, "But I don't want you to talk to him just yet. Let me get some information first and then I'll let you talk."

Chanel leaned up against the wall with a look of caution as I answered the phone. Robert and I talked for a few minutes. He apologized for his outburst during our earlier conversation. He said, "Yes, I do know Virginia and she gave me the message you left on her answering machine." Robert and I decided to connect via Facebook and e-mail. As we chatted on Facebook, I suggested he looked at the photos of Chanel. He quickly responded, "She doesn't look like me, that's not my daughter." I explained to him that fetal alcohol syndrome causes certain facial characteristics, and not all children look like their parents. We exchanged a few e-mails and were continuing to get to know each other when all of a sudden Robert abruptly blocked me from his Facebook friends list. This was the reason I didn't want to tell Chanel about any of this until I was sure Robert and Sue wanted a relationship with her. I was so upset with myself I let out a few tears.

I decided that being honest with Chanel would be best. It would sting at first but she had to know. As I entered Chanel's room she was sitting on her bed all balled up. I knew this wasn't going to be easy. After I told her about Robert's reactions, I did my best to console her but she just wanted to be left alone at this moment. I tried to explain that it must have been hard on Robert, after 22 years of not knowing he had a daughter, for us to come out of the woodwork like this.

"He needs time to digest this," I told her. "You are his only child, Chanel. Let's give him time to absorb this life-changing news. I have a feeling he will call back in a few weeks. We just need to give Robert some time."

We hadn't heard back from Michael and Sue still hasn't called. I was determined to find her on my own so I could talk to her myself.

Since I didn't know what her married name was, this wasn't going to be easy. I looked on Facebook, and searched the Internet's many online phone books, and many other places. It was Classmates.com where I found a listing for Sue's birth name, along with her married name. The operator gave me a phone number for Sue using her married name. I quickly called and a young girl answered the phone.

"May I speak to Susan, please?" I requested.

I could hear the little girl call out, "Mom, someone wants to talk to you!"

"Hello, who is this?" asked Sue, "Hello, Susan," I said, "My name is Sondra, and I believe I adopted your sister. Her pre-adoptive name was Elizabeth B."

"My sister? No, no, I don't have a sister that was adopted out. I think you have the wrong person."

"Is your mother's name Christine?" I asked.

"No, I'm sorry, but you have the wrong person, I don't have

a sister that *was* adopted out and my mother isn't Christine," she insisted.

"I'm sorry, I didn't mean to disturb you, I'm just trying to help my daughter find her natural family."

"No problem," Sue said, "I do know there is another Susan out there with the same last name as me, but I don't know where she is. If I find anything out I will give you a call."

I hung up the phone only to find myself thinking, "That *WAS* Chanel's sister, I'm sure of it. But I can't figure out why she wouldn't want to talk to Chanel." She had the same first and last name, and she lived close to where Christine said she lived in one of her notes. It was too much of a coincidence.

On January 9, 2012, Chanel had a speaking engagement in Clearwater to speak about fetal alcohol syndrome to two different groups of pregnant teens, her "target audience," as she told me. I helped her set up the easels and posters and get her laptop computer ready. One by one the teens came into the class, all looking exhausted. Some looked very pregnant and others didn't look pregnant at all.

I had the privilege of introducing her, "Good morning ladies and gentlemen, it is an honor and a privilege to be able to introduce you to Chanel Torres. She

Chanel speaking to a class of pregnant teens in Clearwater, Florida. After this class she found out her birth mother died many years ago.

is here to talk to you about fetal alcohol syndrome. Chanel is on a mission to put an end to this 100% preventable birth defect and she speaks from personal experience. I am sure that you will all learn a lot from this very courageous young woman. Chanel, come on up!"

The teens were sitting erect and paying attention to every word Chanel was telling them as she struggled through her stuttering. Her speeches are always informative, but were an eye opener especially for this group. She even got the group to laugh at some of her unfortunate experiences. She has a sense of humor and really uses it well to connect with her audience. Once again I found tears in my eyes as if I had never heard her speak. She just knows how to get to your heart strings and tug at them a bit. At the end of her speech she held her routine question and answer session. While the teens asked Chanel questions, my mind drifted to how I was going to tell Chanel about my conversation with Michael and about her mother's death. "Will she cry? How can I tell her in a gentle way?"

After her second presentation was over, Chanel and I packed up our things and headed to the car. As we were about to pull out of the parking lot, I looked at Chanel and said, "Honey, I have something to tell you."

Her eyes looked sad as she replied, "Why do I get the feeling this isn't going to be good?"

I began by telling her about Michael, Susan's father, and our phone conversation. She interrupted me, excitedly asking, "Did you find my sister, Susan? Did you? Did you?"

"I'm not sure, honey," I continued. "I spoke to a Susan B., but she told me that she doesn't know a Christine.

Michael said he would get in touch with your sister, Susan, and give her your phone number. I do have something to tell you about Christine," I paused and took a deep breath, "She died back on January 21, 1995."

Just as I feared, Chanel broke into uncontrollable tears as the news hit her hard. She curled her legs up and cupped her hands over her face. It was extremely painful for her to hear that her birth mother was dead. She wanted so much to share her success story with Christine. "She stole my dreams. I wanted to show her I can survive and now that won't happen." Chanel continued to cry during the ride home and requested to sit in the car by herself after we pulled into the garage. I left her there for awhile before I checked in on her again. For the next few days Chanel retreated to her room and spent most of the day in bed, bundled up in her favorite pajamas. The early stages of grieving had begun, and as her family we were all there to reassure her and help her get through this sadness. Something magical happened after three or four days of grieving. Chanel walked out into the living room dressed in her business attire, her hair in a neat little bun at the back of her head, holding a pile of papers in her hands.

"Where are you going Chanel?" I asked.

"I'm going to advocate for babies, Mom. The one thing my mother didn't take from me was the ability to advocate. I don't want another child going through what I face each and every day. Mrs. Wilson is picking me up in an hour and I'm going out there with my head held high as I educate as many people as I can. I want them to know about the dangers of drinking alcohol while they are pregnant. Even if they plan on giving their babies up for adoption, Mom, they can stop drinking for nine months, just nine, I know they can do it. I will pour my heart out to them."

On January 11, 2012, I decided to write to Sue, the woman I had spoken to on the phone since I had not heard from her and Michael hadn't called back since our last conversation. Along with my letter, I sent pictures as well as a list of Chanel's wonderful accomplishments. I hoped this would inspire some curiosity and a desire to know this amazing woman Chanel. I even asked her to Google "Chanel Torres FAS" to view all the wonderful awards she has won. I waited to hear back from her. Weeks had passed with no phone call or return letter. I came to the conclusion that it was time to give up looking for a bit.

CHAPTER TWENTY-FOUR:

CHANEL'S RISE TO FAME

On January 25, 2012, Chanel burst through the door after school "Mom!! Mom!! Look, look at this!! I'm so excited. Someone came to my school from the Pinellas County Schools communications office, and they wrote an article about me!"

I was so proud I couldn't even find the words to express. "Chanel is a power house," I thought, "There is just no stopping her! She LOVES what she does and can't get enough of it."

I had now become her agent, and she would jokingly threaten to fire me if I didn't give her what she wanted. I wanted to shout it from the rooftops:

"I JUST LOVE THIS INCREDIBLE, UNIQUE, INSPIRING, GORGEOUS, YOUNG WOMAN!"

Chanel was a miracle, evidence that anything is possible—achieving events that are commonly believed to be unattainable for a child with fetal alcohol syndrome. She simply acted upon the things she believed were possible.

It was days like this when I was reminded of Chanel's earlier days, when her home-based early intervention teacher warned me about adopting a baby with fetal alcohol syndrome! I could still hear her words, "Sondra, you have such a lovely family, think hard about adopting Elizabeth. Fetal alcohol syndrome children are very disruptive to families. When they become teens they are troublesome and can cause severe disharmony in a once-cohesive loving family such as yours. She will probably not develop intellectually, and will need constant supervision throughout life." I took these words seriously, and the sadness that poured through my body, charged every inch of my being with confusion, and palpable pain. Little did I know at the time these words would also become the fire behind my motivation to give Chanel the love and support she would need to live an amazing life, beyond the limitations of FAS!

Chanel and Mrs. Gyulveszi, Chanel's mentor from Richard L. Sanders School

The article read:

ADVOCATE IS A YOUNG HERO
AND A NATIONAL AWARD WINNER:

Chanel Torres, Extended Transition student at Richard L. Sanders school, is on a mission to help others who are living and dealing with fetal alcohol syndrome (FAS). She is tireless in her efforts to educate others about FAS and the fact that this syndrome is preventable. She has created a website, www. advocatefortheunborn.com and spends a lot of her time giving presentations at public speaking engagements, facilitating young adult support groups, and working on her autobiography that she hopes to soon publish.

Despite her daily struggles of stuttering, trouble concentrating and learning, and difficulty with writing from living with FAS, Chanel's compassion and determination to empower and advocate for other young adults with this disability has won her national and local recognition. Chanel is a 2012 Yes I can! Award winner from the Council for Exceptional Children in the Self-Advocacy category. She also is a Pinellas County Schools' 2012 Young Hero Award winner.

Chanel is self-confident, expressive, passionate

and professional in her presentations because she chooses to use her life's experience as a person with fetal alcohol syndrome as a teaching tool in the hope of abolishing this preventable syndrome.

This information was given by Barbara Shannon, psychologist at Richard L. Sanders School.

This article was posted on the Pinellas County School website, along with this addition:

Thursday, 26, January 2012 12:28

Chanel goes on to say:

It is caused by the mother who chooses to drink alcohol while she is pregnant. The growing fetus inside the mother is continuously bathed in alcohol for months. The results of the mother's selfish acts

Chanel and Mrs. Shannon, Ed.S, NCSP, School Psychologist - Pinellas County Schools Extended Transition Program

are a baby who is prematurely born with low birth weight, feeding problems, respiratory distress, and under developed lungs. The other problems that continue throughout the child's life include tremors, stuttering, trouble concentrating and learning, lack of memory causing problems to reoccur often.

Chanel sums up her will to continue advocating for the unborn, "The more people I can educate, the more babies I can save from this awful syndrome and suffering. This is my story. This is my life."

I'm an avid Facebook reader and contributor, and on February 9, 2012 I was posting all the wonderful things Chanel had been doing to educate on fetal alcohol syndrome. Suddenly I glanced up and noticed a friend request from Sue. My heart started thumping and I wasn't sure if I should run and tell Chanel or check this out first. "She's been hurt enough," I thought. I accepted the request and for the next few hours I checked into Facebook incessantly until I received my first private message from Sue, which just read "Hello."

I replied immediately, "Hello Sue. How are you? Thank you for requesting to be on my FB friends list. I'm about to leave for work now. I can't wait to talk to you."

The next day, I sent another Facebook message to Sue,

> "Hello Sue, I'm not sure where to begin. I'm not even sure you are who I think you are, sorry, just being cautious, and trying to make my daughter's dream come true. I will look for you when you are on and we can chat "live time" on FB chat. Thank you again for requesting to be on my friends list!"

I received this reply the next day, February 11, 2012,

"I am who u think. My mother was Christine. I can try to call u if you let me know when you are available- I understand the unpredictability of an RN schedule. I am looking forward to speaking with you and appreciate your caution-as you know my father had the same fear. My husband and I, and even my father are very impressed with your daughter's website. She seems like an amazing young woman- I know that we have you to thank for that and even if we never meet I want you to know how thankful I am that you were able to provide the home and family that my mother was not able to. Let me know your work schedule and when is it a good time to call-during school hours are best for me but I can make evenings work to."

I replied, "What a beautiful note above, it sure did tug at my heart strings. Chanel is a powerhouse and is acting on her dream of getting EVERYONE educated on FAS. I work Monday through Thursday and yes, school hours are best at this end as well. I can't wait to talk to you. I'm a bit confused, I will explain when we talk, I sleep during the day and boy I'm lucky to be able to go into a DEEP sleep while the kids are at school but I do miss many phone calls and some important ones. If you give me an idea of when you will call I will keep myself alert and listen for your phone call. If I don't answer that's probably because when I'm not home sleeping during the day I'm at All Children's hospital with one of our children…My second home. This is a quiet week for me, a rare treat so any time any day this week just let me know.

On February 13, 2012 my cell phone rang and when I quickly looked at my caller ID I saw that it was Sue D. We talked for about 20 minutes. Sue explained that she had some health issues and hadn't been able to call Chanel sooner. During this conversation I found out that the packet I mailed out to Susan D. a few weeks ago was sent to the wrong Sue. Although they have the same first and last name, Sue (Chanel's sister) lived in different state.

Sue continued to tell me that she was the one that had to clean out her mother's apartment after her death from a fall. Sue was only 19 years old at the time. As she was cleaning she found Chanel's (Elizabeth's) birth certificate. At first she was baffled and didn't know who this little girl was. She was never informed about a sibling. Sue moved up north to live with her father at the age of nine and stayed there until she enlisted into the United States Air Force.

Soon after finding Chanel's birth certificate, Sue found some pictures of Chanel. Her immediate reaction was, "Oh my God, this baby has fetal alcohol syndrome."

Sue's medical training as a nurse helped her to recognize the facial features of a fetal alcohol syndrome child. Sue said that she hadn't wanted to call sooner because, "I don't want to cloud Chanel's thoughts with my bad memories of our mother." As we continued to talk, I asked Sue if I could read the last letter Christine wrote addressed to Chanel. But when I lifted my mattress to reach for the letters, they were gone. I frantically searched for the letters; positive I had put them there. I recited from memory what the letter said and ended the conversation.

I was sure that my friend Carolee had been right and that Chanel had found the letters. I now had no choice but to tell her about the mission I had been on. Later in the day when Chanel came home from school I confronted her in her room and asked about the letters. I was upset because I had wanted this to be a surprise! Chanel admitted to taking the letters and handed them back to me. She stated she only wanted to read them and planned on returning them from where she took them. She was very sincere with her apologies, and it was obvious. I made copies of all the letters and gave them to her for her records. Now, I had to call my confidant Carolee and listen to her "I told you so's."

Later that day I sent this message to Sue on Facebook:

"Sue, I truly TRULY enjoyed our conversation earlier today. About Chanel and her bilateral cervical rib, doctors have asked us if any other family members also have a cervical rib. Of course we told them we didn't know. If Chanel misses just ONE dose of her meds, the pain is sooo unbearable, she curls up in a ball and cries. The pain radiates into her neck, shoulders and chest area, sometimes down her arm. It wasn't discovered until shortly before her 21st birthday. It's not really noticeable to the naked eye, but boy let me tell you if by accident someone touched that area of her shoulder, the pain is intractable. Chanel usually will not take pain meds other than Advil for fear of her mother's history of addiction being passed on to her. The reason I am bringing this up is perhaps you might have a cervical rib. It's worth looking into since you said you have pain in your neck and shoulder area. Again thank you soooooOOo much for the phone call this afternoon"

I received this response on February 14, 2012:

"Thank you for the info-I will take all I can get to figure out what is going on. It is very challenging to be in pain and have people look at you like you are crazy. With everything I am going through my dad has admitted to me that while he was able to keep my mom somewhat sober while she was pregnant with me, that he would travel a lot for work (he was a truck driver) and he is pretty sure she didn't behave while he was gone. Though she probably didn't drink like she did with Chanel. While I would never compare my life to what Chanel has gone through I can understand her inability to find the right words, to be unable to control your anger and to say the wrong things at the wrong time-many ADHD and cognitive symptoms.

I am looking forward to meeting Chanel, and though I cannot promise a visit in the near future, if you change your mind and want me to talk by phone or e-mail I am here.

I will get a package of Chanel's stuff together to send this week. If you would like I would be happy to include some pictures of myself and my family."

I wrote back on February 14, 2012 :

"OMG you are amazing!! GOSH! Yes, of course the pictures of your family would be WONDERFUL!!! Take care of yourself, then we can move on to step two. I am getting a packet ready to mail to you. I'm even enclosing the letter that I wrote and mailed out to the wrong SUE! I can only laugh about it now! LOL and there is NO changing my mind! If you could have seen Chanel's face when I told her "I think I found your sister" only to find out....wrong SUE!!!!! I can't wait for you to get the packet... I will be picking up pictures from CVS later and hope to mail everything out by tomorrow."

Sue and I continued to talk via Facebook for the next few days, and then on February 25, 2012 we arranged that Sue would call Chanel at 2:15 p.m., just after she arrived home from school. I was so excited, but I kept it to myself because I still hadn't mentioned a word to Chanel about my conversations with Sue. At 2:00 p.m. Chanel's school bus pulled up. Chanel entered the house saying that she was tired and, wanted to take a nap. 2:15 p.m. just as promised, Sue called. My video camera was on and ready to record the event. I called out to Chanel, "Chanel, come here, someone's on the phone for you!" She meandered into the living room and sat on the sofa as I handed her the phone. "Hello, this is Chanel."

I whispered, "Chanel, who is it?" As if I didn't know.

She replied, "Sue," as she shrugged her shoulders, not realizing who Sue was.

"It's is your sister, Sue," I explained. This news caused Chanel to stutter more, and the tears began.

"Um, oh my, God, you don't know how much (stuttering), this is just happy and sad, and all my emotions are coming out, this is just very exciting for me." Chanel stammered over her words with excitement as the tears continued to flow. The conversation went well and they made a promise to each other to stay in touch. When they hung up the phone, Chanel called just about everyone she knew to tell them the good news. For the next few hours Chanel was in a superior mood as she danced around the house. Later that evening, Chanel communicated with Sue on Facebook. She began to ask Sue many questions about their mother. "I didn't even know you existed until our mother died," Sue told Chanel. Shortly after discovering the pictures and birth certificate, Sue called the Suffolk County Department of Social Services Adoption Unit and inquired about Elizabeth (Chanel). She was informed that this baby was adopted into a family that has also adopted other children with special needs and that was all the information they could give her. Even at the young age of 19, sue had been ready and prepared to adopt her sister, but once she heard about her new family she knew that wouldn't happen.

Chanel and Sue talked several more times that week. Sue revealed to Chanel that living with her mother was hell. For a time, the two of them were homeless. "Mom would drink everyday and get drunk," Sue informed Chanel. When she was drunk she used vulgar language and was very controlling. Life was very difficult. Despite Sue's struggles, she earned her nursing credentials as an ARNP in pediatrics, and has been an inspiration to Chanel since this union. Sue is a living example of something I read many years ago and repeat to Chanel every now and then: Our background and circumstances may have influenced who we are, but, we are responsible for whom we become.

Chanel's speaking career and advocacy were just getting started. She was committed to reducing the number of babies born with fetal alcohol syndrome. I knew that the sky was the limit for her. Watching her speak, I saw how dedicated, open and honest she was about her personal experiences while living with the wrath of a preventable birth defect. She has already motivated and inspired so many including myself. She has touched many lives and will continue to do so. During her speeches she captivates her audience with her tenacity and openness. Chanel always had a "no holds barred" Q & A session directly after her speeches and did her best to answer all questions.

Chanel was in high demand as a speaker and enjoyed teaching others about fetal alcohol syndrome. Some of her audiences have included students at the University of South Florida, principals, counselors, high school students and others. She has spoken to a group of ESE teachers from Pinellas County School District at the administration building in Largo, to a group of teachers from other counties, middle school students, high school students, nursing students, PACE, a program for girls at risk and experiencing difficulty or conflict in school or at home, and the list goes beyond what I can remember.

On April 2, 2012, this article by correspondent Sylvia Lim was published in the Tampa Bay Times:

"From being teased to teaching others, Pinellas schools honored Young Heroes, including a former student who struggled with a disability" Chanel Torres stutters and was often teased about it in middle and high school. She never thought she had the courage to speak publicly because of this impediment. Not anymore- Torres now tours the county to give presentations on fetal Alcohol Syndrome or FAS. "I learned that my audience needs to hear the stuttering," she said. "My mother drank when she was pregnant with me. That is where the stuttering is from. "
Torres, 22, was one of three young people recently recognized by the Pinellas county School District with a Young Heroes award for overcoming adversities and giving back to the community.

In her speeches, Torres tells teens and adults what FAS is and how it can be prevented. Then she shares her story.

Her birth mother was an alcoholic, which caused her to be born prematurely, weighing about 4 pounds and 3 ounces. She cried in a high-pitched tone for years.

She was diagnosed with FAS and was given up for adoption when she was 2.

"I will never fully get over my disability, but it's the way that I have learned to deal with the disability that makes me stronger," she said. "Every time I go on a presentation and I stand in front of a group, it's just my way of forgiving my mother for drinking while she was pregnant."

Torres' efforts to educate people about FAS in the past few years have won her the local and national "YES I CAN" awards from the council for Exceptional Children, in addition to the Young Heroes award.

But Torres is quick to note that she's not doing this for the recognition.

"I do it to advocate for children who can't speak for themselves, for the unborn and for the kids that have it," she said. "My disability does not define who I am. I just live with it and I want to teach others how to do it."

On April 12, 2012 the suitcases were lined up at the front door as Armando and Chanel prepared for a very important trip to Denver, Co. Chanel had won the 2012 National "Yes I Can" award for self-advocacy. This was a very prestigious award, indeed. The previous year she had won the local "Yes I Can" award and was nominated for the Nationals. I was so very proud of this young woman, my daughter Chanel. She has struggled her entire life and continues to struggle with behavior and learning issues related to fetal alcohol syndrome.

An accomplished young woman, Chanel was now able to recognize when her behaviors were not acceptable. Her behavior issues will never go away, but with the right intrinsic tools that we had instilled in her, she could now manage these episodes. We had taught her different calming techniques that worked most of the time. Her Yoga lessons, in particular, were very beneficial when the everyday stressors took over.

Chanel and Armando flew to Denver so Chanel could receive the National 2012, "Yes I Can" award in the self-advocacy category and returned on April 15th. She was more than exuberant, with lots of pictures and stories of all the wonderful people she met on her trip. Her pets had missed her and greeted her with wagging tails and squawking.

On April 16, 2012, Gina McQueen from Bay News 9 in Tampa called to request that a team of cameramen come and shoot a segment with Chanel for "Everyday Heroes" With Bill Murphy. The show profiles those that make a positive difference and are an inspiration to others in our community. The session lasted about 45 minutes. Chanel was really nervous and stuttered often. She wasn't expecting the cameras because I just told her it would be an interview. Chanel needed to psych herself up for cameras.

At the end of the session, Bill Murphy commented to me, "YOU SHOULD WRITE A BOOK!"

On the evening of April 29, 2012, we welcomed a new addition to our menagerie of pets. Betty Davis was a mixed breed dog that we adopted from the Dade County animal shelter. Chanel's love for animals had continued to keep her busy. She was a great pet owner and kept their cages immaculate; sometimes she drove me nuts about it.

On May 26, 2012, Chanel gave her first speaking engagement at a juvenile detention center in Pinellas County. I had arranged for her to speak to a group of boys aged 13-17. I didn't tell her that many of these boys were gang members, for fear she would be too nervous and would not be able to speak. The session went well. Only one boy was removed from the room for sleeping. At the end of the session a few of the boys thanked Chanel. Not one of the boys had known that alcohol was dangerous to a fetus. As we were packing our things into the trunk of the car, Chanel thanked me for not telling her beforehand about the boys being gang members.

On June 13, 2012, Rosina headed off to camp Boggy Creek for a week, while the rest of the family traveled to Hallandale for a visit with my brother, Willis, my mother and my sister, Brenda. Chanel and I were looking forward to a speaking engagement I had arranged with the superintendent at the Broward County Juvenile Detention Center. As we pulled into the parking lot of the detention center, Chanel's nervousness and excitement was evident. She wore her usual business like attire with her hair in a neat bun at the back of her head. I continued to be so very impressed and proud of her! She truly loved giving these speeches, especially to her target audience. One by one the boys were escorted into the room with their "bebop" like walk. Some quickly glanced at Chanel and gave her an intimidating smirk just before they were seated. The warden spoke first, admonishing the boys to be respectful; anyone who misbehaved would be escorted out of the room, he told the boys in a firm and authoritative voice. My brother, Willis Morgan, was seated in the far back of the room, Chanel sat directly in front of the boys and I sat just behind her. I gave a brief introduction before Chanel stood up and started her speech.

One of the boys in the front row started to laugh and make fun of Chanel because she was stuttering. He was quickly ushered out of the room, but this only made Chanel more nervous and the stuttering became progressively worse until she eventually collected herself once again. Through it all, she held her head up and continued on. Chanel was determined to bring attention to FAS and she would not let her stuttering get in the way.

She began by reading the letter Christine wrote to her many years ago about signing the adoption papers. The room was completely silent as the boys hung onto her every word. She had made a connection with these boys, who were between the ages of 13-17. Some were gang members, some had FAS themselves and others were undiagnosed but suffering from fetal alcohol effects (FAE). She continued to tell them how she struggles every day of her life, all because her birth mom made some bad choices. I'd heard this speech hundreds of times and yet each time it tugged at my heart as if it were the first time I was hearing it. At the end of her speech Chanel had her Q & A session with the audience. Just before parting, a few of the boys thanked Chanel for her bravery and others apologized for the misbehavior of the boy that was escorted out of the room.

After packing up all the equipment Chanel faced me and said,

"Mom, IF I SAVED JUST ONE BABY TODAY, THEN I HAVE DONE MY JOB."

Chanel and I were a team now.

On July 2, 2012, we were invited to appear on "a local," live radio show hosted by a health enthusiast in St. Petersburg. For the past few days we had been going over the material we would cover. We knew this stuff; it had become part of us. This was an opportunity to get our message out to a much larger audience. At 1:45 p.m. sharp we walked into the small radio studio and met with the host and his producer. He sensed our nervousness and tried to calm us. Well, mostly me, after all, Chanel had been doing this a lot longer than me; she was a professional speaker. We were both happy to be there, although it was a very different forum from what we had done in the past.

For previous speaking engagements, Chanel would prepare a written script and read from it, as well as ad-lib some of the material. But for this show it would all be from memory, with only an occasional peek at the cheat sheets we had laid out on the desk. When I looked at the host during the live interview I got the feeling he was disappointed with how it was going, and that made me more nervous. When the show was over, I was so proud of Chanel. She had done a fantastic job, with very little stuttering.

As we left the studio, the host bid us farewell as he gave us a final note that the show would be converted to a podcast and published on the website for future listening. Weeks went by but the show was never uploaded as a podcast. I felt so sorry for Chanel, especially since I believed it was me who hadn't done well, and that I had spoiled her chance for reaching a much larger audience. Luckily many of my friends and Chanel's followers had been able to catch the show when it aired live, and all praised Chanel for her good work.

CHAPTER TWENTY-FIVE:

CHANEL
MEETS ROBERT

I programmed my cell phone to "bark' when there was an incoming call. On July 11, 2012, I was rushing around the house when I heard the barking off in the distance. I ran to get my phone before I missed the call. I immediately recognized the name on the caller ID. It was Robert F.H., Chanel's birth father. We have not heard from him in several months.

"Hello, who is this?" I ask, already knowing the answer.

"Hi, Sondra, this is Robert. Listen I would like to talk to Chanel, if that's okay with you?"

"Oh my goodness, Robert!" I exclaimed, "Wow, of course it's okay. She would absolutely love to talk to you."

"I have been checking out all the awards she has won, I am so impressed, and she is a remarkable young lady. I saw the one on YouTube for the 2012 National Yes I Can awards, and the one from BayNews 9 for the Everyday Heroes award video that you posted to your wall on facebook. I also saw all the other awards. You must be so proud of her."

Robert and his family

"Oh yes, she is remarkable. Can she call you tomorrow?" I ask.

"Okay, its set. She can call me tomorrow at 8:30 a.m. before I go to work," he agrees.

Chanel made the phone call to Robert just as we had arranged, and I videotaped her as she was on the phone with him. They became fast buddies, and both agreed to do DNA testing as soon as possible to confirm their relationship.

On July 24, 2012, we were like two little kids who couldn't stop smiling at each other with excitement as we drove to the Bay Care laboratory for Chanel's DNA testing. They swabbed her cheek thoroughly and told us the results would be ready in four to six weeks. When we got back into the car Chanel called Robert in New York to inform him she was done at the lab. Much to our surprise, Robert told Chanel that he had just completed his DNA test in Jamaica, Queens. The two of them were so excited and expressed their desire to have the results much sooner. "What will I do for six weeks?" Robert chuckled.

As I sifted through my e-mails on July 30, 2012, I noticed one from Contact@dnacenter.com. This is what it said:

Thank you for choosing DNA Diagnostics Center for your paternity testing needs. We are pleased to inform you that all samples have arrived at our laboratory and testing is complete. The report(s) is now available online. You will be able to access the reports for 90 days from the date the report is issued.

My plan was to keep this quiet until after Chanel fixed her hair and put on her favorite outfit, so I could record her reaction as it unfolded. But I just couldn't keep it to myself for even a minute. I shouted, "Chanel, come here, the results are in!"

She opened her bedroom door with a bang and ran excitedly into the dining room with her hair a mess, wearing funny-looking mismatched PJ bottoms and carrying her lap-top. Frantically, we both tried to download the results without success. After some help from the help line, we got to see these results:

PROBABILITY OF PATERNITY — 99.99998 %

Chanel jumped up and down asking "Mom, Mom, what does that mean?"

"Robert *IS* your father!" I excitedly replied. This is what she had been hoping for.

"Can I call Robert? Can I? Can I call him?" she shouted with excitement.

Her conversation started out, "Hi, Daddy! Hi Daddy!"

I could hear Robert giggling as Chanel told him the results. This was wonderful news. Chanel and Robert had already been talking frequently on Facebook and by e-mail as well as on the phone, and they were building up an adorable relationship. Later, Chanel also made contact with Robert's sister, Nancy R., who she also talked to on Facebook and by phone, developing an equally captivating relationship. Each time Chanel got off the phone with either of them she'd call out, "GOSH, I LOVE THEM!"

As I've said, I'm an avid Facebook user and contributor. One of the groups I visit is called "Flying with Broken Wings." It's a support group for anyone who has a child with fetal alcohol syndrome, knows someone with the syndrome or even has the syndrome themselves. It is also open to just about anyone with an interest in this subject.

On August 14, 2012, I was deeply moved by a post from a woman whose experience I could really relate to; she has adopted children with fetal alcohol syndrome.

She wrote:

> BB:
>
> I am feeling very frustrated, my husband works very hard earning a living!! He is a wonderful husband and father. We spent a lot of money renovating our home. We painted all the walls, new flooring and yesterday bought a new bed for our daughter…guess what? There are already holes in the walls and the bed is broken… not even 24 hours old. We are losing our minds and our money. I understand that they have no concept of the value of things but the lack of

respect is killing me. I am feeling so ....
arggggggggggggggggggggggg!!!!!!!!

My youngest is on her third pair of eye glasses
in only 6 months, she's hard on her clothes and
our oldest breaks things that don't mean anything to her but are MY life treasures...Can
someone please help us!!! We are not a wealthy
family but we try to give our children the best.

I replied to BB:

OMG I know EXACTLY what you're talking
about!!!!

I showed the post to Chanel and she wrote this response to BB:

CT: I did broken my room set 3 times on the
3 time my mom told me you ARE NOT GET-
TING ANOTHER. SHE SAID THAT 4+ years
ago. I learned not to do it again don't buy them
another bed so they will learn not to do it again.
I know that it may not work but give it a try.
Visit: Advocatefortheunborn.wordpress.com

There were other responses as well:
TVN wrote:

We simplified our life. Nothing out that mat-
ters if it gets broken, our living room curtains
got so much abuse that I made half curtains so
they can't be used as a swing; it makes it easier

on them and us. Adapt the environment so it works for everyone, even if it is a mattress on the floor.

VS added:

> I just put the mattresses on the floor for Tori. She hasn't "broken" the bed yet, but the constant jumping.... I know they aren't TRYING to destroy things, but she just doesn't seem to get the "boundaries" all the same and it has reduced the stress levels on all sides. I have a couple mission cabinets in my room that I keep special treasures in. I keep it locked with a zip tie through the handles. I also keep things that she REALLY needs to stay out of in my office and keep that room locked. There are many very nice STURDY pieces of furniture that can be found at flea markets extremely cheap and I let her decorate them to her taste with washable markers or paints. It gives her something to decorate and keeps the walls "safe". Just a couple of ideas. Good luck, I feel your frustrations.

BB:

> The original poster on this site wrote back to say:" I don't have space in my home to lock things up, their mattress was on the floor and they have been through 2 box springs already. I

am feeling very overwhelmed!! Everyone tells me it gets better with age but I find that it's getting worse. Feeling very upset! Sorry!!! I guess I am taking their frustrations personally and don't know how to deal with it.

R.J.F replied:

Well, this may be kind of old fashioned and Draconian. But if they get an allowance make them pay for the damages.

BB wrote:

They don't get an allowance for that reason!!! We give them money when they earn it!!! Not a weekly allowance.

MK wrote:

Our son's door has been broken for over a year because when we put him in his room he kicks it. I decided not to get a new one until these outbursts stop

This was from FB:

Hello Ms. BB, we built platform beds using plywood and 1x4s and don't use a box spring, we built beds into loft style but on the floor, both my sons and my daughter have holes in the wall from the door handle L, my son...well, destroys stuff. I know it's all in just play, I just sweep up the mess every so often and throw away, something's one simply has to accept, other things lock up, I have to hide things to keep them safe, tools are a problem they disappear.

BB ended with:

Thank you to everyone…not feeling alone but still a little frustrated…I used some of my respite today to recharge my batteries…thanks again!

I wish there was a support group like this when I needed someone to talk to, who understood exactly what I was going through. Participants from this group pour out advice from personal experience, just like family.

Meanwhile, Robert and I had been talking secretly and making plans for him to surprise Chanel with a visit. He was scheduled to arrive in Florida on October 14, 2012. I wasn't sure exactly how the surprise would unfold but I knew it would be good.

Finally the night arrived, Sunday October 14th; Robert called me on my cell phone to let me know he had arrived at the Comfort Inn, a hotel that was not far from our home in St. Petersburg, Florida. Robert's wife Virginia was with him. I could hear the excitement brewing in his voice. Our plan was that Robert would drive to our home, knock on the front door and pretend to have a delivery for one of the children. He arrived sporting a large black cowboy hat and sunglasses and held a medium-sized box in his hand. He knocked loudly and I yelled out for Chanel to answer the door. She quickly walked over to the door and peeked out to see who it was.

"It looks like a delivery," she yelled out to me as she opened the door.

It just took a split second for Chanel to gasp and realize that it was her birth father Robert standing in front of her. We were all astounded at how tall he was. Hugs were exchanged.

Robert, Chanel and Armando
"my DADS"

Chanel hugging on
her bio "dad"

The next few days were devoted to Robert and Chanel getting to know each other. Chanel and I treated Robert and Virginia to a visit at Disney World. When we returned, Chanel was all excited to show Robert our old family videos of her growing up with the Torres Family. Chanel read the very last letter she received from Christine to Robert. I could see how moved Robert was by that.

Signing with a Heavy Hand and Heart

At the end of their visit, Robert presented Chanel with a very beautiful gold and aquamarine necklace that had been sent from Robert's mother, Elsie. Chanel plans to call Elsie in the near future to thank her for the beautiful gift.

To date Chanel has not met her sister Susan, but they do keep in touch via e-mail, text messaging and phone calls.

Robert putting a necklace on Chanel from Grandma Elsie.

Robert's sister Nancy Chanel has become very close to Nancy and they talk often

Robert and Chanel having lunch at Disney World

Robert reading the letters from Christine for the first time.

FINAL NOTES

:

To date, Chanel continues to have behavior issues although not as severe as before; she will continue to need some supervision for the rest of her life. She now recognizes what triggers some of the behaviors and can avoid them. Luckily the issue with the sticky fingers and many of the previous issues have been resolved for several years now. What Armando and I have done is to help Chanel recognize when something is inappropriate or wrong. At times these warnings enter Chanel's thinking process too late, but we are much further along today than we were a few years ago.

We have found out that in Chanel's case, medication was not the answer. The arguing in her room has resolved as she grew older and her brain integrated slowly. Raising her has been a treasure beyond belief, full of surprises, twists and turns, along with great potential. I often wondered what Chanel's life would be like if Christine hadn't exposed her to alcohol prenatally. Would she be able to fulfill her dreams of becoming a veterinarian, driving a car, getting married and owning a pet shop?

Chanel is very articulate, and intelligent in her own way. In some areas her skills are above average, and in other areas they are below average. She has an extremely hard time getting her thoughts onto paper, as you have seen from her notes in this book. Yet many people she has met cannot initially tell there is anything different about her, even after talking to her for 15 minutes or so. She no longer has that sign across her forehead that reads: "FAS." She has grown into the facial features that were so identifiable when she was younger.

Armando and I will not take all the credit for the great person Chanel is today. Chanel has had a great support system from her schoolteachers, counselors, neighbors, family and friends as well as one doctor in particular, her pediatrician, Dr. Cimino. We are forever grateful for his help with guiding her in the right direction. As a team we have maximized her many strengths, such as: taking care of pets, working with computers, cooking and speaking publicly about fetal alcohol syndrome. We have taught her to think first, and to take her time. We have minimized the negative effects of fetal alcohol syndrome. Although we have been through a bumpy road with Chanel, we are so proud of whom she is becoming.

Chanel continues to be a delightful, lovable, charming and mischievous young woman. It's ridiculous how much we love her. I hope that along our journey together we have set good examples for her to emulate, as we strived to lovingly support Chanel in all her endeavors.

I want Chanel to know that as she begins the journey through adulthood in a world full of peer pressures and bullying from the ignorant and uninformed, I will stick by her through the tearful sad moments, the good and wonderful, the happy and the unpredictable times.

An adoption contract is FOREVER!
To my beautiful Chanel, with **love, Mom**.

Sondra

22 years of schedule books with diary like entries

CHANEL'S FINAL LETTER TO CHRISTINE

Dear Christine.

I never really know you but I know that you are my birth mother and that you were sick. I wanted to ask you so many questions that I will not be able to ask you all of the questions that I needed to ask you. When I found that you died it was hard for me. Some of the questions that I needed answered I got answered from Sue and Robert. Living with a 100% preventable disability. I don't think you knew that you were hurting me. I know you loved me. I am glad that you gave me up. I have to live with what your drinking did to me. But because of what you did to me I have learned to live this way. I don't want to live this way but I have to. Some of my dreams will never come true. Your drinking has made me live very very hard. I was teased in school. Through all of what I have been through I have learned to forgive you. A lot of my time spend teaching others not to drink while they are pregnant. I was very mad at you for giving me FAS but as I started to learn about FAS and you, I started to forgive you. I have a very hard time with math, spelling, and getting my thoughts onto paper. It was bad that you had to hurt me with your drinking but why did you have to drink with Sue? I know that it was not a lot. I think Sue is madder at you then I am. You loved both of us, what mother doesn't love their children. If I would of meet you I don't what I of said to you. I just wish you could see what I am doing with my life. This is where I become I will keep advocating for all of the unborn babies. I just had to get my augur out.

I live with a great family now. My mom made you a promise that she would take good care of me and she has been taking great care of me, I don't know where I would be without her.

From Chanel

Do you need
a motivational speaker?

CHANEL TORRES

Council for Exceptional Children

2012 National Yes I Can! Award Recipient

Pinellas County Schools 2012 Young Heroes Award Recipient

Bay News Nine Everyday Hero Award Recipient

Chanel Torres is a powerful speaker who shares her personal story of living with Fetal Alcohol Syndrome (FAS). Her mission is to prevent alcohol use during pregnancy. Her role as a disability advocate began in 2008, when one of her teachers asked her to speak to her classmates about Fetal Alcohol Syndrome.

Ms. Torres has since spoken to teachers, guidance counselors, social workers, administrators, students and community groups regarding the dangers of drinking during pregnancy, not merely through statistics and facts, but through the eyes and experiences of someone who lives with FAS daily. She is tireless in her efforts to educate those around her about FAS and its prevention. Ms. Torres demonstrates such passion, initiative, and dedication toward her goal, that despite daily struggles, she eagerly and actively engages others in her mission to eradicate FAS in her lifetime through public speaking engagements and education. She is in the process of writing her autobiography, is a member of the Pinellas County Schools Family Life Education Speakers Bureau, and is available for speaking engagements suitable for students from Grades 6-12, parent groups, educational professionals, community and civic groups.

Words from Ms. Torres:

"I take my FAS and turn it in to a teaching tool to help others learn what I go through every day of my life."

"If one person listens to what I have to say, then I have done my job. This is what I was born to do. I have won many awards for my work. The awards I've won have been great, but my biggest award is knowing that my message is being delivered and knowing that I might be helping so many people and unborn babies. . If I can prevent one more child from this awful syndrome I will be happy. My ultimate goal is to get the word out there that FAS is 100% preventable. I want everyone to know about the effects of alcohol on the fetus. My advice, my plea, is that you PLEASE, PLEASE do not drink while you are pregnant, even if you plan on giving your baby up for adoption. Let your baby fulfil his or her dreams and live a normal life. For all the fathers to be, you play an important role in this too. You must be encouraging and supportive. Staying away from alcohol yourself would be helpful."

WHAT OTHERS ARE SAYING:

As always I continued to be amazed by you. You are brave, inspiring and dedicated and have embarked on a wonderful journey. You have not only embraced what you have endured but have became the biggest and strongest advocate for those who come behind you and most importantly to the prevention of FAS. I am proud to know you and look forward to reading your book in its entirety.

With great admiration,
Heidi D'Ambrosio

"*Ms. Torres is a true light in a world that needs more education on Fetal Alcohol Syndrome and its effects on unborn children. She has opened doors that will never be shut. She has just begun to educate the nation on Fetal Alcohol Syndrome.*"

Deborah Thornton,

SEDNET Project Manager

"*Ms. Torres is the epitome of self-advocacy and embodies strength, resilience, and determination. She is courageous and tireless in her quest to educate others regarding FAS; and is compassionate and determined in her mission to empower and advocate for other young adults with disabilities.*"

Barbara Shannon,

School Psychologist

CHANEL TORRES IS AVAILABLE
FOR A SPEAKING ENGAGEMENTS
TO BOOK THIS SPEAKER FOR A PRESENTATION,
PLEASE GO TO:
Advocatefortheunborn.wordpress.com
or call (727) 576-7684

Made in the USA
Charleston, SC
17 August 2016